LOCAL GOVERNMENT
IS IT MANAGEABLE?

A Critical and Up-to-date Assessment of Local Government
Operations with Examples and Explanations

Other Titles of Interest

BOTKIN, J. et al.
No Limits to Learning: Bridging the Human Gap

COLE, H.
The British Labour Party: A Functioning Participatory Democracy

FITZGERALD, R.
Human Needs and Politics

FRIEND, J. & JESSOP, W.
Local Government and Strategic Choice, 2nd Edition

JOHNS, E.
The Social Structure of Modern Britain, 3rd Edition

JOHNSON, N.
In Search of the Constitution

KHOSHKISH, A.
The Socio-Political Complex

SOEN, D.
New Trends in Urban Planning

WENK, A.
Margins for Survival: Overcoming Political Limits in Steering Technology

LOCAL GOVERNMENT
IS IT MANAGEABLE?

A Critical and Up-to-date Assessment of Local Government
Operations with Examples and Explanations

by

L. GORDON BAYLEY

B.A. (Com.), M.Sc., F.I.O.B., A.M.B.I.M., A.C.I.Arb., F.R.S.A.
Councillor, Stockport Metropolitan Borough Council
University of Manchester Institute of Science and Technology

PERGAMON PRESS

OXFORD · NEW YORK · TORONTO · SYDNEY · PARIS · FRANKFURT

U.K.	Pergamon Press Ltd., Headington Hill Hall, Oxford OX3 0BW, England
U.S.A.	Pergamon Press Inc., Maxwell House, Fairview Park, Elmsford, New York 10523, U.S.A.
CANADA	Pergamon of Canada, Suite 104, 150 Consumers Road, Willowdale, Ontario M2J 1P9, Canada
AUSTRALIA	Pergamon Press (Aust.) Pty. Ltd., P.O. Box 544, Potts Point, N.S.W. 2011, Australia
FRANCE	Pergamon Press SARL, 24 rue des Ecoles, 75240 Paris, Cedex 05, France
FEDERAL REPUBLIC OF GERMANY	Pergamon Press GmbH, 6242 Kronberg-Taunus, Pferdstrasse 1, Federal Republic of Germany

First edition 1979

British Library Cataloguing in Publication Data

Bayley, L Gordon
Local government, is it manageable?
1. Local government - England
I. Title
352.042   JS3111   79-41224
ISBN 0-08-024279-0

In order to make this volume available as economically and as rapidly as possible the authors' typescripts have been reproduced in their original forms. This method has its typographical limitations but it is hoped that they in no way distract the reader.

*Printed and bound in Great Britain by
William Clowes (Beccles) Limited, Beccles and London*

Contents

Preface

Since 1966 I have been elected to serve on three different local authorities: an urban district, a metropolitan county and a metropolitan borough council. I have also been concerned in my working life with management practice. The views expressed in this book are a result of marrying experience of private industry with that of the public sector. Many will not be surprised at the contents and in particular at some of the criticisms, having held suspicions of such practices and procedures. Others, including some councillors, will dismiss them as irrelevant mutterings of a member of a minority party. Unfortunately a book of this nature can never be comprehensive, for as each meeting takes place, some other aspect is unfolded.

It is my fervent hope that all who are involved in local government will study the book with care. Some suggestions might not be acceptable, while others need implementation to ensure that some of the practices recorded are not being repeated elsewhere.

The student of local politics will undoubtedly be able to identify areas for further investigation, and research is needed to improve and develop some of the techniques and suggestions made.

It is impossible not to be engaged in public service without making friends amongst officers, as well as members of all parties. It is this friendship, born of mutual respect in spite of very differing attitudes and practices, which offsets much of the frustration of not being able to achieve enough because the power to change has been with one or other of the major parties. I value these friendships, and while some may be able to identify themselves, I trust that they will be forebearing with me as instances known to them are cited to illustrate various points.

I owe a special debt of gratitude to many people, not least those of my present neighbourhood, who have expressed their confidence in me four times. To my own party and in particular to our 'jury' of one good woman and eleven good men on the Greater Manchester Council, I owe a special debt for the experience they accorded me as their leader.

No one can enter public life without sacrifices and my family have been patient in allowing me to pursue political activity. Their help over the years is very much appreciated. For patience with my writing, my congratulations go to Mrs. Christine Davis for typing much of the original draft, and to my wife Gwen who typed the final manuscript.

June 1979

Gordon Bayley
72 Hill Top Avenue
Cheadle Hulme
Cheadle, Cheshire

CHAPTER 1

Re-organisation or "Who Paid the Price?"

The arguments about the wisdom of reorganising local government in 1974, brought about by the Local Government Act 1972, will be debated for another decade at least, particularly by those who had experience as a ratepayer or as a councillor in the former urban or rural district councils. It is these people who are best able to compare the sense of community which was so often a feature of the former small authorities with the increased impersonality and remoteness of the new larger boroughs and districts. Those who lived in the old municipal and county boroughs which now form part of the metropolitan counties experienced little change, except that in many cases the relatively impoverished poorer central areas were joined with the more affluent suburban areas. In the shire counties, the new districts are geographically so big that the sense of community has tended to be destroyed except in those cases where parish councils formed out of the former urban and rural districts have flourished. How long these newly-formed parish councils will continue to generate a community spirit is open to speculation. At present much of the enthusiasm comes from those who were the councillors of the former district authorities. Now that their powers are seriously curtailed, frustrations could soon become evident.

It was inevitable that a major change of this magnitude would bring losses as well as gains. Whether the erosion of the former sense of community has a lasting effect on the quality of life only history will judge. There have been some serious attempts to provide community and neighbourhood councils to re-generate the sense of community. But initial enthusiasm has already waned in some instances, with few people offering themselves for election to such bodies. The reason probably lies in the growing apathy in the face of greater centralisation of power, together with the sense of frustration at the lack of powers which can be exercised by these councils. Where these councils have been established in new suburban areas, the transient nature of much of the population, who are in the middle executive range, has not helped to provide continuity of membership.

The Local Government Act 1972 was designed to make local government more effective and could have been used to devolve some of central government's powers, at least to the new counties. Instead reorganisation meant a shuffling of powers between the new two tiers of local government, much to the hostility of the former single tier county boroughs. Reorganisation may be viewed historically as one of the wasted opportunities to make local government more accountable to the people. It did in fact the precise opposite by removing the former municipal Water and Health Authorities from democratic control by elected persons. Instead of elected persons

1

to serve on water authorities and health committees, there was a new batch of
appointees, partly by the Secretary of State and partly by the constituent local
authorities, so extending the gift of political patronage still further. Such a
situation provides an opportunity for political corruption. It could in time make
such bodies an arm of central government through its directly appointed personnel.
There are already signs of this happening which means that the extent of democratic
control has been seriously eroded. It is a drift in a direction over which the
people have not been effectively consulted and which adds yet another nail in the
coffin of the notion that government is for people and not for the political parties!

Clearly there are tasks which local government has to fulfil which are best done at
local district level. These include housing and social services, whereas transportation policy needs a broader canvas than that available on a district basis. It is
noted, however, that the shire counties operate the social service and the educational functions whereas in the metropolitan counties they are a district responsibility. Already there is some discussion on a revision of these functions. In the
case of the social services it is suggested that districts should have greater
influence, and that education should revert to some of the former large county
boroughs which were absorbed into the larger districts within the shire counties.
In some ways the latter proposal implies a move back towards the pre-1974 division
of responsibilities.

It is not intended to enter into a discussion about the boundaries of the new authorities. It is inevitable that whatever boundaries were drawn up, there would be
anomalies, especially where special pleading was successful in re-drawing certain
boundary lines contrary to the original plan. As a result some of the decisions
appeared to be based more upon emotion than on logic. This is the price that must
be paid for having a democracy.

Local government has never been known to act swiftly, having developed for a variety
of reasons, its own inertia. This is so very different from private enterprise
that the prospect of having to act with speed sends shivers down the spine of most
public administrators. Therefore, the haste with which re-organisation took place
brought with it many acute problems. Many councillors and officers worked extremely
hard in the interval between the passing of the Act and the first elections to the
new authorities. Of this there can be no doubt. But the speed with which the
selection procedure for the staff had to be implemented certainly denied many authorities the opportunity to sift out the merits and demerits of the applicants,
since so few had experience in working within the large organisation created by the
Act.

The limited time to give effect to reorganisation certainly prevented the formation
of really sound policies for the major areas of activity. This was not a problem
for those cities such as Manchester whose boundaries were almost unchanged, but
where enlargement based on an existing large town took place, the relevance of the
former policies was not evaluated at the time of formation. As we shall see in a
later chapter, the introduction of corporate management, so essential in the enlarged authorities, was being carried out in a very amateurish fashion resulting from
the fact that so many officers, as well as councillors, had little or no experience
not only of corporate management as such, but also of being involved in such a
large undertaking as these new authorities. It will take many years before true
corporate management is fully operative. Unfortunately when personnel are in such
protected employment as local government, the task of weeding out those to whom a
corporate involvement is an anachronism is both too slow and cumbersome.

Local government has always been under close scrutiny. In 1967 the committee on
'The Management of Local Government' reported. It is worth looking at some of the
recommendations made nearly twelve years ago.

1. The work is fragmented between too many separate departments and these are
seldom coherently organised or led by the Clerk.

2. Each Authority should appoint a clerk as undisputed head of the whole paid
service of the Council.

3. There is too wide a gulf between governors and governed.

4. The taxing powers of local authorities must be strengthened, and the dependence
of local government on central finance reduced.

5. Local authorities should be given a 'general competence' to do what they think
necessary for the good of the people they serve.

6. Seventy should be the maximum age for standing for election.

It is pertinent to ask how many reports, study groups, etc., are needed before
some or any recommendations emanating from them are implemented, or are they just
reports prepared for the sole benefit of students of political science?

The 1967 report was followed by the decision in May 1971 of the Secretary of State
for the Environment together with the various local Authorities Associations to
set up a study group on local authority management structures in anticipation of
the passing of the 1972 Act. It was chaired by Mr. M. A. Bains, Clerk of the Kent
County Council. Its report was titled "The New Local Authority's Management and
Structure", since when it has become known as the Bains Report. The report recognised the unique opportunity to re-examine the management structure; in doing so
it concluded among other things that the "traditional departmental attitude within
much of local government must give way to a wider ranging corporate outlook".
This particular matter is a thread which runs through the subsequent chapters. The
corporate approach to the management of local government affairs is of equal importance to elected members as it is to the officers themselves.

The Bains Committee, whose membership comprised local government officers with one
exception, noted that chief officers are 'skilled men' trained specially for the
work of local government. There are few chief officers whose technical and professional skills are in doubt, but their training for the task of management is
conspicuous by its absence. It is this failure to understand and appreciate management in its full corporate context that results in some of the appalling waste
of effort and resources within local government to-day. It arises out of a lack of
awareness of the need to establish managerial accountability and to monitor managerial effectiveness.

We next come across the Committee's conclusion that "the Council .... should
alone have a role as a policy formulating and detailing forum". Strictly speaking
this is a valid conclusion. Unfortunately policy formation requires research and
a considerable expenditure of time to develop. It cannot be left therefore to the
elected members to undertake this preliminary work. They are not paid to do it,
few if any are equipped to do so, in addition to which their time is very limited.
Therefore it falls upon the officers to do this preliminary work. Unfortunately,
it is equally true for the private as well as the public sector that top managers
spend too little time in policy formation and too much dealing with to-day's, and
more especially yesterday's problems. The immediate problem-tackling process
creates a sense of activity, while planning is a thought-provoking process. The
former is often viewed as productive in contrast to the latter. Further, policy
formation is not part of the training and experience programme of many local
government officers. What is disturbing, is the fact that so many officers will
not accept the truth of this statement. Ask departmental chiefs for a policy

document which guides the operation of their departments, and they will provide
numerous pieces of paper with ad-hoc statements uncorrelated to any corporate
function either within their own departments or more particularly within the authority itself. Further, if my assertion was not true, there would not have been the
floundering experienced at the genesis of the new authorities in April 1974, as
councils searched for some corporate identity.

A special chapter is devoted to the role of the chief executive, suffice it to
comment at this stage that the Bains Committee recommended "Each authority should
appoint a chief executive to act as leader of the officers of the authority ....."
Such a reference to leadership without stating that he should be the head of the
council's paid staff to whom the various departmental chiefs should be responsible
underlines perhaps a serious omission in the Committee's report. It is indicative
that the Committee, composed almost exclusively of those from local government,
failed to appreciate the true nature of management and of corporate management in
particular. In consequence, the subsequent reference to the 'establishment of a
management team' has been taken up as an alternative to a truly executive role for
the council's chief officer. Without the emphasis on the executive role of this
officer, the creation of management boards has in many instances lead to their
deterioration into talking shops on trivia if their agendas and reports of their
deliberations are anything to go by. Alternatively they have directed their attention to establishing a consensus approach to policy submissions to the elected
members rather than directing their attention to the management of the policies
already determined. The admission by some chief executives as to their lack of
managerial training explains why the present state exists, although reorganisation
was an opportunity to change this. It only bears out the adage 'you cannot teach
old dogs new tricks'.

The Bains Committee stressed the need to have an effective personnel management
function, commenting on the fact that local government prior to 1974 lagged behind
private industry in its recognition of the true function and development of
Personnel Management. Even to-day this aspiration has still not been fulfilled.
It is common to find appointees responsible for this function without any formal
training and guidance. It is as if there is a notion that a person who is socially
acceptable must be competent in the personnel field. Sometimes the management
services function based on organisation and method study assumes a greater pre-
eminence than that of the personnel management function. It is indicative that the
role of personnel management must assume a greater importance, due to the problem
of managing the enlarged local government units.

One of the major recommendations of the Bains Committee was for the establishment
of joint meetings of district and county members to co-ordinate the interaction of
the functions and policies of the two tiers of government. Stockport has implemented this recommendation with the establishment of an area committee system whose
membership comprises councillors from both tiers. However, such an arrangement
remains unrecognised by the county council which still stands in splendid isolation
within its brick castle, indifferent, it appears, to the needs of its residents
where the functions and policies of the two tiers interact. The fact that so few
authorities have adopted the Stockport model of the area system, or a variant of it,
is a commentary on the state of development of local government at the present time.

The public is disenchanted with reorganisation. They valued the ease with which
they could make contact with officers who were often members of the community. It
was inevitable that there would be a move towards centralisation under reorganisation. However, some authorities set up local information offices which have
provided a very valuable source of contact with the general public. These offices
often cover a smaller area than that of former district councils, which tends to
make these contacts more local than hitherto. Stockport is a classic example of

this, where their offices are located within the communities, providing a very useful source of information on a wide range of topics, including tourism, social
security benefits, leisure activities, etc. However, such centres do not entirely
overcome some of the organisation problems created by greater centralisation of
services in enabling residents to contact the officers responsible on matters of
concern to them.

Very few district councils have effectively operated an area management organisation. Many shire counties have done so for a number of years. Metropolitan
districts are smaller in geographical area than the shire counties and probably
considered that there is little need. The failure to provide area management has
been another disappointment of reorganisation, since it has concentrated rather
than diffused decision making, besides removing the sense of identity with the
community which a localised area organisation can engender. It requires a highly
developed managerial structure which pushes responsibility for performance lower
down the hierarchy. Local government chief officers seem reluctant to delegate
managerial decisions to effect council policies.

It was inevitable that when new authorities were created around the large towns
that the core of the officers would be drawn from the largest authority within the
area. Firstly, because they had experience of large organisations and secondly,
to all intents and purposes, they were already in the post! Whether they would
have been able to cope with the managerial problems of the even larger organisations remained an open question. Clearly a number of staff from the former small
authorities did not like the environment of a larger authority, and many able
people with a considerable length of service still to give did retire on the very
generous terms provided under the 1972 Act. Not only was there in some instances
a severe loss to the community, but it was also at a considerable cost in terms
of pensions, etc. Some, however, remained on in the public service even in a consultancy capacity, others who were employed in posts which carried a lesser salary
enjoyed protection of their former salary. This protection still exists some five
years later in a limited number of cases.

There were the odd exceptions to the concentration of the new metropolitan
districts around a former county borough. One was Tameside in Greater Manchester,
where there were five municipal boroughs with no focal centre amongst them. This
has created organisational and community problems which will take many years to
resolve. Because the new metropolitan counties were new creations centred round
the largest city in each county, it was natural that the officers would tend to be
drawn from the central cities rather than from the former smaller constituent
authorities. This situation applied in the case of the Greater Manchester Council.
There was also the political leadership problem to be resolved. Again the experienced politicians from the large former cities took over the leadership role. The
former city members formed a very strong clique which transcended political parties,
at least as far as their judgement as to the method of establishing the organisation for the new county councils. The elected members of the major cities met
during the daytime, and the metropolitan counties tended to follow this practice
which suited those members who served on both tiers of government. In consequence
there was a reluctance amongst businessmen to offer themselves for election to the
new county councils.

In the case of Greater Manchester, there was one constituent borough, Wigan, which
had all the appearances of an old type pocket borough in that it returned a solid
block of labour members. It wasn't long before the Wigan members were christened
the Wigan Mafia. This turned out in the end to be a most unfortunate impression,
not because there were some very able members who could in no way operate mafia
techniques, but because it diverted attention away from the effective mafia, which
with hindsight could be viewed as operating through a combination of officers and

members of all parties who served in the pre-1974 era on the Manchester City Council.
The title mafia is not to imply anything corrupt, but a close grouping of officers
and members who from long experience of each other transferred the Manchester modus
operandi without the opportunity to breathe a breath of fresh air into the system.
For four years, it was sufficiently strong to lock out of the inner sanctum of
officers, a director of a department who happened to be the only non-Manchester
man. It was also a clique which the second chief executive, chosen from outside,
had to face after the initial appointee had retired. Yet in spite of this empathy
between officers and members from the former city, they were unable to cope with
the relationships necessary between them and their successors in the revised
Manchester City Council.

The fact that the officers came from former constituent authorities was not without
some benefits. Since the chief officers were known to each other and had worked
together, there was no need for in-fighting to establish an order of precedence
amongst them, or even a reputation! This had been established during their period
of service within the former authority and it did spare the new county council from
such disruptive actions. However, it is essential that the 'in-breeding' which was
a feature of these first appointments should be positively counter-balanced by
barring internal promotions on retirements, etc. until some new blood is brought in.
Having no experience of other metropolitan counties it is impossible for me to
judge how much the Greater Manchester Council's experience was mirrored elsewhere,
although I suspect that it is unlikely to be unique.

The new members drawn from the former rural or urban districts often found an
injection of petty party politics which has been totally absent in the former districts where party politics were confined to a very few major issues. Nowadays
every attempt is made by some minority parties to use local issues for the purpose
of debating national policies. This is particularly true of the labour party in
Stockport. It could well be repeated elsewhere. This is an appalling waste of
time and a misuse of local government, since it distracts attention away from the
real local issues. When local government is often viewed by the ambitious as a
stepping stone to a seat in Parliament, such diversions are used by prospective
parliamentary candidates as a vehicle for a public relations exercise, and in some
cases to impress their own party members with a view to adoption for a particular
constituency.

Nothing can really be devised to overcome this abuse of local government except
for the party leaders to rescue debates and to remonstrate with the offenders.
However, one must not be unmindful of the fact that there are some shrewd political
manipulators who at times do welcome such diversion of attention away from local
contentious issues! This whole intermingling of national policies with local
issues is now a fact of life within the new authorities, but whenever it is carried
to excess it can alienate those officers who are deeply concerned for the local
community, and worse still it can have the serious effect of alienating the elected
member from the paid official who has to witness such exhibitions.

The use of the provision in the Act to protect earnings created a suspicion that
some of the former authorities failed either to effectively monitor staff or to
overpay them! Unfortunately time was not on the side of those making the appointments in 1973 in preparation for April 1st 1974, to scrutinise past performance too
carefully. In consequence, it was possible for a less than adequate senior
officer to suggest as his or her subordinate those whose capability matched his or
her own level of performance! Some departments still suffer from this situation.
A number of appointments were made where some of the junior appointees have exhibited greater capabilities than those in senior posts. This has not helped efficiency and has created within the staff ranks a certain amount of hostility towards
certain officers as well as considerable frustration. Such situations arose out

of the virtual guaranteed employment provided by the Act, which if re-employment was impossible provided the employee with very generous compensation.

The protection of earnings provisions covered manual workers as well as staff. The complications created by different bonus schemes and special local payments operative in the former constituent authorities meant that attention had to be paid to a procedure for producing a standard scheme which would apply to new entrants. It is inevitable in such situations for rounding-up rather than rounding-down to occur by buying out the former practices. This has undoubtedly substantially increased the cost of local government reorganisation and was reflected in the rate levy increases in the early years of the new authority's existence.

Overtime was considered in certain cases to be protected! The amount of overtime being worked in the G.M.C. in certain departments was of alarming proportions. Reports were received of employees who were receiving very substantial salaries, doubling their earnings due to overtime and week-end working. This matter will be discussed again in relation to the activities of the District Auditor in Chapter 13. The longer the practice of paying these additional payments continued, and the longer the new authority delayed detailed investigations, the stronger became the argument that such payments accorded with the custom and practice of the new as well as the former authority, and were part of standard conditions of employment for such personnel. Management became more and more impotent as the concept of corporate management failed to be implemented. It might almost have been seen to be a deliberate corporate policy not to disturb the tranquility of the status quo.

Many personnel employed by the former smaller authorities were highly competent within the constraints of size of those organisations. Their translation to similar posts in a larger authority meant that some floundered badly and still do. The 'Peter Principle' of 'appointing persons beyond their level of competence' was more prevalent than many people in local government are prepared to admit. There is an assumption by senior officers that he or she is a competent selector, and once the appointment has been made, those who did so are reluctant to admit their possible failure at the selection process. The position hasn't changed to any marked degree since 1973 when the first appointments were made.

It is clear that local government has cost the country millions of pounds, at a time when shortly afterwards we entered a disastrous period of inflation. The major cost arises from the increased cost of labour employed by councils. Since the chief officer's remuneration is geared to the rateable value, it is not difficult to see that all chiefs (except those where the boundaries were little changed) enjoyed enhanced salaries with the consequent roll-on effect to the second and third tier officers and so on down the line! Unfortunately salaries which are increased in this way do not result in any greater competency, especially when old familiar faces re-appear in a new, larger, office.

It is clear that since 1974 the annual increase in the cost of local government exceeds the norm of wage increases of those who have to pay the rates! When this is coupled with the effect of hiving off the old municipal water undertakings to the new water authorities, who are able to prepare grandiose plans regardless of expense, and subsequently surcharge the unfortunate householder, it will not be difficult for future historians to estimate the cost in effective taxation of the 1974 reorganisation. Reorganisation can still bring benefits. But the difficulty of teaching old dogs new tricks and the greater danger that new dogs may learn the old tricks, means that some very serious thinking needs to be done, and the sooner the better if we are ever to recover the opportunity to ensure that reorganisation can ultimately be seen to be a cost-effective exercise. If it cannot, then the case for any further reorganisation must surely founder on the rocks of cost.

CHAPTER 2

Selection of Officers or "The Caretaker Will Tell You"

Some Experiences

The suggestion that the caretaker can have prior knowledge of the appointment to be made is not too remote from the truth in certain areas. I heard of a case in one educational authority area where the caretaker informed a would-be applicant not only that he would be rejected for that particular school, but indicated the one for which he was earmarked! Some would suggest that it was an inspired piece of guesswork! However, there are indications that the access to the educational grapevine may lead a caretaker to be nearer to the truth than many would like to admit.

While it is not universal practice, the drawing up of a short list for interviews can be restricted to a very limited number of people. In some cases, this could be the Chief Officer together with the appropriate chairman and possibly the vice chairman. In respect of the case referred to previously, the full list of applicants was not submitted to the appointing committee.

If the caretaker knows the system of selection it is not difficult to predict the outcome. It arises from the manner in which the short list for interviews is compiled. It is what I describe as the Tory Party selection procedure. It is a simple device whereby at the pre-selection stage by an inner caucus the 'favoured son' is identified. At the official appointing meeting he is not put forward with the second, third or other close contenders, but competes against those who may be sixth and lower in the caucus' pecking order. At the full selection meeting, the 'favoured son' is seen as the outstanding candidate and duly selected; whereupon the selection meeting breaks up with a feeling of euphoria, congratulating themselves on the wisdom of their choice! Incidentally, such a procedure can come a little unstuck. In one well-known by-election the 'favoured son' for a variety of reasons withdrew within 48 hours of the full selection meeting, but it was too late and would have been embarassing, possibly, if they had called forward the second person in the ballot at the meeting of the inner caucus! In such a situation, a more reliable selection process takes place, but the constituency, especially if a safe seat, can be saddled with a less acceptable candidate!

If therefore a pre-selection process on these lines takes place for a headship of a school, the education authority is able to delude the local personages, since such selection panels often include all or most of the governing body, of the wisdom of their choice. Those devising such selection procedures would contend that if there had not been the pre-selection process with the 'favoured son' as the front runner, the result of a closely contested selection could leave too many local worthies, responsible for management of the school, dissatisfied with the choice. At least, they would argue, they all go away content, and knowledge of the overwnelming support is likely to ensure that the head starts with the goodwill of the community! It could simply be a case of the ends justifying the means!

Seldom do the members of such selection meetings appreciate the confidence trick which has been played upon them. When a leading local industrialist was question-ed as to the manner in which a selection panel for a headship on which he served made its choice, he was unaware of the possibility that there had been in effect a pre-selection processfor which he along with others had acted as a rubber stamp. Once it was explained to him, he found everything fell into place.

However, there are grave doubts in such situations as to whether the best available applicants are given a fair chance of selection. But far more important is the power given to the inner caucus, which regardless of the membership can lead to very undesirable practices and a form of conscription.

It is not only the preparation of short lists, which are a matter of concern. The procedure at these committees can be very unsatifactory. In another authority area, I accompanied a fellow party colleague to a selection of a Head for an Infant School. The selection committee mainly comprised members of the Divisional Educational Committee, who were members of the County Council. The meeting was opened by the Chairman asking the members to make comments on the written applic-ations before us. Not many questions were raised at this stage for both of us decided we wished to discuss the application form in the light of the interviewee's performance. The Chairman then invited the applicants for interview. To the first, she asked what she knew of the Plowden Report, which had very recently been published. The applicant appeared to be in ignorance of its recommendations. Whether this influenced the chairman as to the wisdom of expecting teachers to be so up-to-date or not, I do not know, but she never asked any of the other applic-ants that particular question. This seemed to be bad practive from the start, and as the proceedings continued grave doubts entered my mind as to the reason for that particular question being asked of the particular applicant. It was left to others, not members of the Divisional Executive, to probe deeper. Unfortunately the Chairman never explained the manner in which she was going to conduct the interviews, possibly because she expected members of her own divisional executive to be familiar with the procedure!

There remains a lasting conviction in my mind that the chairman was significantly inexperienced in selection procedure but above all, she had certain questions lined up to point the panel towards her (and presumably the officers') own pre-conceived choice! However, the unsatisfactory procedure didn't stop at the interview stage. Once the interviews were completed, the committee was asked to vote for their preferred choice. Protests that some of us wished to discuss the merits and demerits of the candidates were overruled by the chairman on the grounds that this was not the procedure adopted by the County Council! As a protest both my colleague and I declined to take any further part in the selection process, believ-ing it to be a farce. We were subjected to abuse for allegedly being unco-operat-ive! With hindsight, it was a farce as well as a travesty of justice, born out of the possible twins of inadequate knowledge of selection procedures and of nepotism.

These experiences and accounts together with recent involvement in appointing officers on re-organisation of local government leads me to the conclusion that a number of authorities need to revise their selection procedures as a matter of urgency. It was clear once local government re-organisation became a fact with the election of Shadow Councils in 1973 in preparation for the take-over from the former authorities on 1st April 1974 that the first most crucial appointment would be that of the Chief Executive. Although there had been working parties consider- ing various matters, comprising representatives from those authorities due to be absorbed within the new units, which had carried out some preliminary planning prior to April 1974, appointments were not within their remit. However, prelimin- ary lists of applicants to the various posts had been drawn up and were available for use by the newly elected councils. Since the new County Councils had been elected a month before the new District Councils, the former were able, if they moved speedily enough, to take the pick. This would be expected anyway since the County Council posts carried larger salaries than was the case in the Districts.

While some who had served on the various working parties were duly elected at the subsequent elections, there were a large number of new faces, and in particular of councillors inexperienced in operating within such a local government organis- ation. Yet such was the need to expedite appointments, especially by the numerous District Councils if they wished to secure the best available material, that little or no basic discussion took place on the proposed structure of the authorities in the light of the Bains Report, particularly as far as it related to the initial appointment of the Chief Executive.

A few of the former authorities had embraced the concept of a Chief Executive; most had continued the former practice of having Town Clerks or Clerks to the Council who were best described as "chief amongst equals". Yet the role of Chief Executive was conceived with the objective of injecting into the authorities management's task of directing and controlling the totality of the Council's operations, besides bringing with it a corporate rather than a departmental approach. Many councillors and officers nurtured in the former local authority structures contended that the former Clerks were the nearest approach to the idea of a Chief Executive and therefore were seen as the appropriate persons to short- list for such appointments. The regulations governing the re-deployment of staff consequent upon re-organisation sought to avoid redundancies and required their deployment with the service; accordingly the opportunity to appoint from outside local government service was lost.

Faced with the need to make this initial appointment of the Chief Executive, there were no readily available man specifications or job descriptions upon which to base ones choice, although the Bains Report did contain a simple draft. It was with this in mind, therefore, that the twelve strong Liberal group on the Greater Manchester Council drew up a specification which it considered to be the basis upon which such appointments should be made. Such a specification was by no means perfect but at least it provided a basis of possible discussion in order that the appointing committee should at least agree on the criteria upon which an assess- ment could be made.

I was therefore alarmed to experience for the first time on such a large Council, having previously served on an urban district council, that not only did the Leader of the Council, who had an advanced copy of the suggested specification, reject any discussion of a job specification, let alone that forwarded to him, but that the larger opposition party had a three line whip on, directed in a negative way to ensure the exclusion of a particular candidate. The reasons for this opposition have never been fully understood, although there were hints that in a former post this applicant had crossed the path of that party over a proposed development which was dear to the heart of one of their members.

The adoption of such attitudes, when officers perform their duty as they perceive it, bodes ill for any appointee in those cases where aspirations of those closely associated with political parties, or who contribute to their funds, are thwarted.

It was also interesting to note that the Leader of that party who is prominent in private enterprise remarked to me that this applicant had been out of local government too long! He had in fact been directing a commercial undertaking closely associated with local government, and under the policy direction of representatives of local authorities. It may be that such a remark was in reality made to justify his opposition to the candidature. Little wonder that appointments to senior posts are bedevilled by spurious factors rather than proven ability to perform as a manager. It is both true and fair to comment that this particular applicant had not only been a Town Clerk, but in his appointment was exercising the duties and functions of a manager in its fullest sense; if managerial ability was considered to be the most important of the criteria for the appointment, then he probably had the broadest experience needed for the task of Chief Executive. It was the failure in this case as well as in others known to me to set out a job description that gave rise to my subsequent doubts as to the wisdom exercised by a vast majority of councillors in the manner in which they set about making appointments.

A few Councils have abolished the post of Chief Executive. Such instances are clear evidence that prior to such appointments, the viable job description together with an appropriate clarification of his managerial role in relation to that of the elected members was never thoroughly researched and established. I have grave doubts as to whether in the majority of authorities to-day they have yet tackled this problem of job descriptions, as we shall see in the next chapter.

It is against similar backgrounds that the selection of the Chief Executive and other departmental heads was conducted in the various new authorities.

The first task was to draw up a short list. It was clear from the brief notes of the various aspirants that there was a limited number of persons with experience of larger organisations from which a possible short list could be prepared. The question arose as to who, if appropriate, to submit for inclusion. Fortunately the majority party left it to members of the policy committee (drawn from all three parties) to submit suggestions for inclusion. Accordingly I undertook a series of discussions with leading figures in Government Service who had a working relationship with local authorities as well as with others connected with local government in different parts of the country to obtain their assessment of the various applicants' ratings. We were therefore able as a group to put forward names for inclusion in the short list. The Chief Executive and the Departmental Heads have wide ranging contacts with national government and numerous other agencies, and therefore an assessment of their performance in these external relationships is important, while for more junior posts it is less applicable.

Looking back on the selection process, I believe that this piece of homework is essential in any appointment. It was still deficient of any information as to knowledge of the ability of the candidates as seen by those within their respective authorities.

The official procedure for appointing the first Chief Executive was based on an application form and a three-quarter hour interview, but very little subsequent discussion of the merits or demerits of the various applicants. Due to the absence of any job description against which it would have been possible to measure each candidates attributes, it was extremely difficult to assess the basis upon which other members of the selection committee were preparing to make their choice, in spite of the fact that the largest opposition party had a three line whip (or so it appeared) directed towards the exclusion of a particular candidate! This was not helped by the apparent desire of the Chairman and a few others to curtail discussion. When the convenience of selecting applicants who are personally known to members of the selection committee takes precedence over other considerations, the qualities of the candidates identifiable from the application form and which they display at the interview take second place. This was apparent throughout a whole series of appointments. In one instance, the application form and the performance at the interview of one successful candidate would have ruled him out from consideration had this not been the case. In another, one officer who was successful in obtaining a more junior but no less important a post was excluded from the short list for the senior post; yet his performance at the interview and his polished application form would have made him a very strong candidate for inclusion on the short list for the senior position!

It is clear from hindsight that the whole procedure was unsatisfactory. It must be remembered however that most members of the new County Councils had either no previous local government experience or had served on various small District Councils. There was however a smaller but highly influential group who had served on the Manchester City Council. This group had the advantage of personal knowledge of the officers of that authority which because of its size was likely to have officers with the requisite experience and qualifications. Consequently, the group wielded considerable influence even cutting across parties!

The selection of a Chief Executive was repeated some years later. On this occasion it was possible to advertise nationally both within and outside local government service. A number of persons from outside local government did submit applications. It was alarming to find that one such choice, who on paper seemed a potential candidate, when interviewed not only had not done any homework, but seemed completely ignorant of the functioning of local government! This person was engaged in Management Consultancy! It may be to be the living proof of the statement 'if you cannot perform, teach, if you cannot teach, consult'!

On this occasion there were three clear first runners. I had a number of discussions with two of them in private to probe their thinking in greater depth than would otherwise be possible at an interview before twenty-one members of the selection committee. This was an invaluable exercise, along with soundings as to possible staff reaction upon appointments and the reasons for such reactions.

Although it was agreed that the committee would be prepared to take all day over the appointments and even have a lunch with the candidates in order to discern more about them in a relaxed atmosphere, it was all over in the space of two and a half hours!

The procedure used for voting is worthy of comment. It is the practise of the labour party not to recognise preference at a single ballot, but to indulge in exhaustive balloting. Initially it was agreed that two of the five candidates should be dropped out of the reckoning. A first ballot took place. If it had resulted in a clear majority, then the clear leader would be appointed. Since only nineteen members were present, the voting was nine for one candidate and five each for the other two. The next stage was the elimination of one of the two who secured five votes each. Here tactics played this part. Who do you vote for if you voted for the front runner on the first ballot - your second choice or your third? Clearly you would vote for the latter to improve the chances of your preferred candidate. The final ballot was ten to nine due to one person switching from the defeated second ballot candidate to the leader of the first ballot. Yet such is fate! If the two missing members of the committee, both of whom were from the party with the three line whip, had been present, the result would have been the other way!

It is clear not only that the use of the party whip for appointments makes a mockery of the selection process, but that the method by which all local government appointments are made leaves too much to be desired and it leaves many questions

that need to be asked of those responsible. The description of these events shows
what is a common practice throughout local government, and one suspects elsewhere
as well. Besides, it is often the case that references have been requested after
the appointment has been made and therefore are not available at the selection
committee!

Use of Job Descriptions and Man Specification

Our draft specification submitted to the Council Leader is set out in the next
chapter, since it refers to the post of Chief Executive. However, it has now become
the general practice to provide job descriptions for a number of posts. While
attempts have been made to follow modern practice used in the private sector, there
are still inadequate job descriptions submitted to the appropriate committees. The
reasons are numerous. There is evidence of inadequate training in the preparation
of job descriptions. Some can charitably be described as sloppy. Many fail to
identify the prescribed tasks and the areas where the office holder is expected to
exercise discretion. One document which purported to set out job descriptions for
posts in a re-organisation of a department demonstrated as a result of an interrogation that the descriptions were totally inaccurate, and had not been devised
from the series of standard procedures needed by that department to fulfil its
duty. Another job description for a second-tier officer stated "that he/she was
to ensure that the corporate budget and plan met the requirements of the departmental budget and plan". Little wonder that it is stated that in local government
the tail wags the dog! Yet such gross errors are being made by officers who are
being paid very substantial salaries!

Inadequate descriptions also arise due to the fear that they might be too rigid
and lead to the possibility of bargaining for re-grading. It is clear that at any
point in time the duties are clearly known and therefore should be spelled out.
It has also been known for descriptions to be used as a device, at a particular
point in time, to enable certain duties to be transferred from one officer to
another, due either to inadequate procedures being discovered, or to a desire to
demote (or move laterally) an individual with an inadequate performance.

I have known job descriptions to be drawn-up prior to the advertisement for a post
without any relationship to what goes on elsewhere in a department.

While local government has its procedures to select staff it has none to "de-
select" them. Its reluctance to tackle this problem is a great barrier to efficient
operation. The mass of appointments made in a great rush after April 1973 increased
the possibility of failure amongst appointees, due firstly to the premature retirement of experienced officers, and secondly to the promotion of a large number,
particularly in the middle management posts, without adequate preparation, experience
and training. Many who performed adequately as fairly senior officers in small
district councils suddenly found themselves bewildered and lost in authorities
five or six times the size of the former ones. Little wonder that the selection
procedures described, and the inadequate, or absence of, job descriptions, led to
serious mistakes being made. These mistakes are still in posts to-day. Unless
local government is prepared to review its structure and in particular the performance of the staff, besides having the guts to take unpopular but essential
decisions to effect changes, the legacy of the disaster of April 1st 1974 will be
with us for many years to come. Worse still, the chances of continued failure in
appointments will persist until job descriptions are treated seriously and the
selection procedures made relevant to modern needs.

Can we improve selection procedures?

There will be no improvement in the selection process until a number of changes

are made. Firstly, reliance cannot be placed solely upon an application form and
an interview. Secondly, greater research in depth is needed into the candidate's
ability to perform. Thirdly, there must be a recognition by elected members that
unless they abdicate their present desire to appoint officers other than the Chief
Executive, they will undermine their own professed belief in corporate management.
Fourthly, the opportunity to cross-fertilise with posts outside the strict con-
fines of local government must be increased. Fifthly, all officers and those
elected members serving on selection committees should be required to attend seminars on the selection process and interviewing techniques. These will be dealt
with in turn.

The first two are inter-linked. Some people are extremely good at an interview
and in submitting an application form. The initial impression, for that is all
that can be achieved under the present system, can be found to be false. The
difficulty arises that since so many appointments are for specialists, elected
members are unable to assess the extent of the specialist's technical competence
and they are often hesitant to make a judgement on such matters. Instead they
base their decision on an impression as to whether they would or would not like to
work directly with that person. The relationship between elected member and
chief officer are but a part of the total job.

A second change is necessary to overcome the greatest weakness of the present
system, namely, the inadequate knowledge of the ability to perform, including the
all-important task of management. Interviews alone are incapable of making any
assessment unless very detailed questionaires are sent to applicants for them to
elucidate their detailed experience. A space on the application form for the
applicant to write his own assessment of his skills is only of value if further
questions and cross-examination at the interview are based upon it. By and large
the listing of referees is of minimal value unless the referees themselves have to
answer a detailed questionaire. The listing of referees at present is to all
intents and purposes part of the "impression stakes" the applicant engages upon
for the name and position of the referee is seen to be of greater importance than
the information provided. In some cases, references are taken out after the
appointment is made. I was once asked to give a reference for a former student
when I was convinced that he had already been appointed to a teaching post in a
state school. The post was for mathematics up to 'A' level standard. A scanning
of his record, however, showed dismal failure in that subject with a somewhat
indifferent performance prior to University entrance!

Most senior posts, as stated, require specialists. Once installed as a departmental chief, the use of specialist and professional knowledge is of less real
consequence for the effective operation of the department than managerial ability.
It is at this level that appointments from outside the local government circle can
be important. One of the most successful and effective departmental chiefs came
not from inside the service but from the armed forces. The appointment of
Nicholas Stacey to be Director of Social Services in Kent was a fascinating
appointment, and clearly challenged the notion that internal service appointments
are considered by some councillors as desirable and therefore inevitable.

It is not easy to obtain an objective assessment of the ability to perform in the
vacant post, but time and effort must be spent by somebody or a small group to
attempt such a thorough assessment. It is possible to see how this might work in
the case of head teachers, in the light of the experiences described earlier.
Would the William Tyndale problem in London have occurred if members of the selection committee had visited the school where the applicants taught and discussed
their philosophy and approach against the background of their former post. How
many other problems involving the Headship of schools which do not make the
national headlines lead to vociferous parents meetings complaining about methods,

discipline, and attainments of schools, which would have been prevented by a more thorough investigation into performance characteristics of the applicant? It is of little value to place too much credence on the knowledge of the Directors of Education otherwise these events would not have occurred. Further, some Directors have not taught in any or all levels of the schools under their jurisdiction, and their knowledge of potential candidates is frequently more limited than that of parent governor/managers of the schools. Further, some Directors in the face of demonstrations from parents either adopt the posture of Pontius Pilate, absolving themselves from any responsibility on the grounds that others made the selection even though they may have - as seen earlier - played a vital part in drawing up the short list. Others believe that there is some special mystique known only to educationalists which entitles them to discount the opinions of those whom they regard as being non-professionals; yet all of us at one time or another have been victims of the educational system and of those who professed to have ability to instruct, guide and counsel us when we were within the system!

It should be standard procedure in the case of selecting head teachers that some members of the panel should visit and report upon the schools of those who are on the short list, provided the panel determined that short list for the reasons shown earlier. Some may recoil at the cost needed to implement this, but the cost of failure to make the right appointment together with the anguish of parents and possible effect upon the children involved cannot be measured entirely in financial terms. How many such visits would have been paid for out of the total costs incurred in the procedure necessary to resolve the William Tyndale affair?

Unless there is power for the selection panel in appropriate cases to "de-select", i.e., dismiss those whom it has selected - a situation which the teachers' unions would resist strongly - the only logical substitute would be for the parents to show their reaction by being granted complete freedom of choice of school, so that those schools where the appointments were unsatisfactory would become empty. However a study of such a step could result in pressure for additional facilities etc., at the successful schools, and this would be a heavy burden to the authority. Yet it must be remembered that private schools survive solely on their ability to perform to the satisfaction of parents. No such pressure exists in state schools where all teachers are cushioned, rightly or wrongly, against the possibility of the parents' reaction to indifferent results. Therefore, one alternative, if the State educational system is to compete with the best in the country, is to establish a more rigorous selection procedure, not only of the head teacher, but also the staff. The other is to have relatively short - say five year - contracts of employment, which are renewable if appropriate.

It is important therefore for councillors and the additional members of the Education committees to resist, in the event of improved research into candidates' capabilities, the suggestion that educationalists are the sole repository of expertise in all teaching methods etc. Such a view begs the humane right of all parents in a democratic society, or one that professes to be so, that they should have some say in the manner in which their children are educated for the life they must lead when independent of immediate family ties.

The third change needed to make selection more effective in local government is for the elected member to accept the role of Chief Executive for what it is in reality conceived to be. The role is fundamentally different from the former role of Town Clerk as chief among equals. The appointment of Chief Executive must be based in the firm belief that he or she is solely accountable to the Council members for the management of the Council's affairs and the achievement of the Council's objectives. The operative word is accountable. When it comes to the appointment of heads of departments, they should in the final analysis be his appointees. It would be incorrect to assume that elected members need have no

involvement. At present the Chief Executive reduces his position on many such
selection committees to that of a committee clerk. I have never known him to play
any significant part in the selection process. It is almost as if by design he
has abdicated his responsibilities of accountability. Yet in a true managerial
structure all officers are ultimately responsible to him. This situation and its
consequences will be discussed further in the next chapter. However, as far as
the selection of a Chief Officer is concerned, all Chief Executives should have
the assistance of elected members in order that in reaching his decision he may
have the views of such members with whom that officer will have considerable
dealings.

It will be difficult for elected members to swallow such a reduced role in selection of departmental heads, but they cannot have the concept of a Chief Executive
without the consequences of corporate management which such an appointment implies.
While reference has been made to the appointment of head teachers, the discussion
about accountability in respect of the Chief Executives has relevance for other
teaching posts. It has been noted that in the case of one council the list of
delegated powers to the Director of Education states that he has powers in consultation with the head teacher to make other appointments to schools. How can head
teachers be truly accountable for the performance of their staff, if some remote
person like the Director of Education takes over the ultimate responsibility for
appointment? I am not suggesting that the contracts of service of the teacher in
a school are personal to the head teacher, nor am I suggesting that the Director
of Education should not have some say, but the ultimate decision must be that of
the Head. How else can he be held strictly accountable for the performance of his
staff? The best managerial practice is to establish true accountability and therefore the best practice of private practice should be the standard of local government.

The fourth change involves the interview itself. It needs more careful structuring
but above all the selection panel needs sufficient time to examine the candidates
thoroughly. It should be standard practice for some five or six characteristics
and attributes to be specified, and a requirement that each member of the panel
puts a score for each candidate against these factors. After the interview the
discussion should turn towards the scores of the councillors and so enable them to
move towards a consensus. At present it is too haphazard to be satisfactory.

The fifth change which is worthy of consideration for the most senior posts is a
panel of external assessors chosen by the authority whose reports can be made
available to the selection panel. This is the practice in the academic world
where it works reasonably well in relation to the applicant's professional standing
It should be stated, however, that since for professorial posts there is no
enquiry or assessment of their managerial ability, some of the problems within
universities can be readily understood!

The sixth change is one of attitude in respect of bringing in outsiders into the
local government fold. It is true that local government operation is equivalent
to the different technologies used by different firms and therefore has to be
learned, but private enterprise has been able to affect switches satisfactorily,
and there are many people with managerial skills who could take senior managerial
posts especially if they have industrial experience akin to a local government
activity like construction work, etc. It could be said that the real danger to
local government competence lies in the fact that the organisation is virtually
totally in-bred, having in the organisational field all the disadvantages of an
incestuous relationship! This can only be broken by a 'blood transfusion' from
outside. Reference has been made to instances where this appears to be a success
but it is often the failures which have made the headlines. The successes are
seldom proclaimed from the rooftops! Yet it is strongly contended that where

failures did occur, the nature of the change, namely the need for managerial skills rather than high technical expertise has sometimes not been accepted by officers and some elected members!

The final change needed is that of training in all aspects of selection. Very few chief officers ever admit that they have something to learn! When training for posts became the vogue after re-organisation with particular evidence of management development, the chief officers in the G.M.C. sent their deputies, shying off undergoing such an experience themselves! By doing so, they exhibited one of the worst traits of those in managerial positions, namely self-deception, by assuming all knowledge, or worse still, an unwillingness to learn or to test ones own state of knowledge. The most important posts are those at the top of a managerial hierarchy and therefore all senior personnel without exception need to improve the selection process and especially the interview. The criticism of officers' lack of skill in selection applies also to elected members with equal force.

It is important, in view of local government's shakey record of effective perform- ance, particularly during re-organisation, that such training should not always be in-house, but provided by some of the very experienced bodies operating in this field outside local government. It has already been said that the cost of failure to make effective selections is high. Using the maxim that 'prevention is better than cure', the local authorities have a duty not to skip the basic groundwork needed to improve the all-important process of selection. Failure in this field makes it all the harder for elected members to do their job effectively, and above all will cause bitterness and frustration from ratepayers at the inadequacies of a bureaucracy incapable of sorting out its own problems and procedures!

One final word on selection concerns the question as to whether there is need for that post. Here I refer to the lower eschelons within local government. Is the post really necessary? Could it be done by others or even private agencies? This goes to the root of the problem but the question still needs to be asked every time there is a vacancy.

CHAPTER 3

The Role or Function of the Chief Executive
— "What's in a Title!"

A number of Councils have decided to dispense with the post of Chief Executive.
It is therefore important to understand what the role and function of a Chief
Executive should be. The new Councils created by re-organisation had as a guide
line a draft job specification set out in the Bains Report (Appendix J). It is
reproduced below:

"1. The Chief Executive is the head of the Council's paid service and shall have
authority over all other officers so far as this is necessary for the efficient
management and execution of the Council's functions.

2. He is the leader of the officers' management team and through the Policy and
Resources Committee the Council's principal adviser on matters of general policy.
As such it is his responsibility to secure co-ordination of advice on the forward
planning of activities and services, and to lead the management team in securing
a corporate approach to the affairs of the authority generally.

3. Through his leadership of the officers' management team he is responsible for
the efficient and effective implementation of the Council's programmes and policies
and for securing that the resources of the authority are most effectively displayed
towards those ends.

4. Similarly he shall keep under review the organisation and administration of the
authority and shall make recommendations to the Council through the Policy and
Resources Committee if he considers that major changes are required in the
interests of effective management.

5. As head of the paid service it is his responsibility to ensure that effective
and equitable manpower policies are developed and implemented throughout all
departments of the authority in the interests of both the authority and the staff.

6. He is responsible for the maintenance of good internal and external relations."

In the previous chapter I referred to the preparation of a specification for the
Chief Executive of the G.M.C. which was denied discussion by the Chairman of the
Policy Committee which was entrusted with the appointment of this officer. In
order that readers may know the basis of the thinking of the group in respect of
this appointment the specification is set out as follows:-

The Chief Executive

A. General

The post of Chief Executive of the Greater Manchester County Council differs from that of a Metropolitan District Council in a number of ways.

1) There will be less direct contact with council members and the public, due to the different functions of the two types of authorities and the dispersion of the members.

2) It calls for a 'man of status and integrity' who can project himself to a wider public.

3) His overall responsibilities will be less concerned with detail but more concerned with concepts and overall developments.

B. Special Duties

The post calls for specialist skills to undertake the following tasks:-

1) To negotiate with:-

a) Government Departments.
b) Industrialists to attract industry and commerce.
c) District Councils to smooth the functioning of the agency arrangements.
d) Other County Councils over mutual problems.

2) To establish a sound corporate management structure.

3) To project a vision for the region.

4) To recruit and develop staff at all levels.

C. Departmental Responsibilities

The Chief Executive should have departmental responsibilities for certain common functions to maintain overall contact and control of the Council's operations. A traditional department will not free him for this task, while isolation will weaken his control.

These direct functions should cover:-

(i)   Personnel
(ii) Public Relations
(iii) Management Services if instituted.

(The secretarial and administrative functions should be combined in a separate department along with the traditional legal functions).

D. Criteria for choice of Officer

1) He should have shown considerable creative ability, being able to have considerable perception of the role of the County within the region. Experience on adaptation will discount any lack of creative zeal.

2) He should be able to formulate the structure and policies of the Councils with these creative skills and serve long enough to bring them to a large measure of

fruition. It is unlikely that anyone whose normal term of service will expire within 8 years of appointment would be suitable. He should see out at least 2 full Councils. As the retiring age for local government officers will in all probability be accepted as 60, no one of 53 or over will be able to meet these requirements.

3) He must exhibit very high personal qualities which will be reflected in his standing with:-

a) Government officials.
b) His equals in executive grades.
c) The respect in which he is held by his subordinates.

4) It is likely that a person who shows evidence of high integrity will be able to show that he is capable of developing staff. This will be evidenced by his ability to attract and train staff of quality.

E. The characteristics which will be expected are therefore:-

1) A personable man.
2) Be creative in intellect.
3) Concise and decisive in speech and writing.
4) Have 'diplomatic' skills.
5) High degree of personal integrity.
6) A sound judgment and ability to assemble relevant facts.
7) Skills of corporate management.

The problem of selecting an officer when the specification and the skills required to assess the merits or demerits of applicants are not even agreed, let alone set down for the selection committee to understand. The choice depended therefore on individual members of the selection committee's own perception of the role and function. If the job specification set out in the Bains Report is accepted, then it is essential that the job specification of the other chief officers is complementary and refers to their responsibility to the chief executive in respect of the efficient management and execution of the Council's functions. There are very serious gaps in this respect in a number of chief officer's job specifications. It may well be the case that where Authorities have dispensed with the post, the concept of accountability of each chief officer to the chief executive was neither expressed in writing or even understood, let alone accepted.

It is the corporate management structure which must stem from the chief executive through the departmental heads to all levels, and be thoroughly integrated in all the relevant job specifications.

Traditionally the professions, whether in local government or in private industry, jealously guard their independence under the cloak of professional integrity. Those who are closely involved in the construction industry are more than fully aware of the attitude of designers who are members of chartered institutions which implies that anything commercial is tainted. Further, very few of them have ever had any management training, some outwardly despise the notion that they should be managed to effect efficient operation of the project upon which they are engaged. This quest for "freedom" from managerial interference applies equally to many other professions employed within local government. The practice dies hard, for the structure of local government prior to re-organisation had committees allocated to oversee departments.

It was in the late 60's that a number of authorities, as a result of publicity and government influence exerted through the newly established National Building

Agency, started to appoint officers with a more corporate role, titling them as
Directors of Technical Services, Directors of Development, or similar. Yet such
a corporate role within the staff structure was not complimented by a committee
structure which sought to plan and monitor progress of the corporate activity.
The problems arising from this will be discussed later.

Pre-1974, where the Town Clerk acted as Primas inter Pares, there were attempts to
provide cohesion in development activity in those cases, where there was no designated director responsible for this overall task, by designating a junior appointment within the Town Clerk's department to co-ordinate development work. Such an
arrangement was seldom effective, for it only paid lip service to the real management task. Such an appointee could only in effect operate as a liason officer
since his status and salary would inhibit any direction and control by him. Such
an approach to the problem demonstrates that neither officers nor councillors had
grasped the significance of the gap between such an arrangement and what is really
meant by corporate management.

Little wonder therefore that on re-organisation in 1974 a large number of
personnel, both at officer and elected member level, who had grown up and who were
familiar with the departmental approach, used such titles as Chief Executive and
talked about corporate management without any real appreciation of their implications, especially since professional independence rather than interdependence
had been so thoroughly engrained in the traditional local government structure.

The Bains report and its adherents were seeking to establish a structure whereby
one person exercised overall responsibility, and was therefore accountable to the
elected members. Faced with the appointment of chief executives with inadequate
job specifications which were often not integrated with those of the other
officers, many new chief executives had little choice but to adopt ruses and to
use their personality to overcome resistance to the acceptance of accountability
through the chief executive to the Council.

There was a clear relationship between increased resistance to such change and the
age of the departmental heads. When job security is so entrenched, as it is in
local government, evolution can take a generation. Unfortunately the need for
effective organisation cannot wait this length of time, more especially when the
enthusiasm of juniors is soon replaced by sheer frustration, so that in the end
the object of most officers is for a quiet life where people work the system and
use it to their own and not the corporate advantage.

It is therefore essential that the titular head of the paid officials becomes a
chief executive in every aspect in the same way and with a similar accountability
to that of a managing director in private industry. This accountability carries
with it the acceptance that failure or inadequate performance in the corporate
function of the authority must mean replacement, something which local government
and, in particular, the appropriate trade union, must also accept. The suggestion
in the job specification set out in the Bains Report that the chief executive
should be a "leader of the officers management team" implies a watering-down of
the role of chief executive as it is generally understood outside local government. It would be unfortunate if the use of such titles in the public service
creates different interpretations as between the public and private sectors since
the majority of councillors will be drawn from those with experience in the
private sector. I believe that Bains did local government a disservice when it
watered down its language on this matter. He should be the Chairman and Director
of that management team, which incidentally should in my view include elected
members. This however will be discussed later. One of the early impressions of
local government, fostered by the service itself, is the notion that local government is quite different from private industry and that it has little to learn from

those outside it. This has bred an isolationism which is proving disastrous to the development of effective local government.

The tasks facing chief executives in the counties and in the districts differ in some respects according to the powers vested in each type of authority, whether it is in the metropolitan areas or in the shire counties. The major difference in powers between the two tiers of government is that of education. The two tiers of government - county and district - carry with it a different emphasis on strategic and tactical skills for the county and district respectively. Both however still require someone of ability to control and direct these activities.

The grouping of the Metropolitan Counties is the nearest this country has come to a more regional type of governmental structure. The Liberal group therefore placed considerable importance on the economic role of the Metropolitan County Council, which was reflected in the specification. The advent of the new Chief Executive shows that this is now appreciated and an organisation established to give effect to this role.

The new metropolitan authorities being substantially increased in size required additional personnel as Chief Executives with the capacity to deal with the problems. The only authorities where personnel had comparable experience were the former larger County Boroughs, the shire counties and London. Unfortunately those from the Greater London Council area were excluded from being appointed to the new authorities. Experience therefore in the former borough was the only guide as far as local government experience was concerned. It was a sweeping challenge, which has not always been successfully met.

The relationship between the various authorities of county and district were complicated by the assignment of concurrent functions and the possibility of the counties using agency agreements with the districts. It is a natural tendency to guard ones own territory with great care. These arrangements, which will be discussed in Chapter 8, are delicate in terms of relationships, both at Councillor and Officer level. Considerable pressure rests therefore upon the Chief Executives of all authorities to safeguard the duties entrusted to each authority for the sake of their own employees and the prestige of the Council members as they see it, yet those concurrent functions and agency agreements require considerable patience and perseverance besides a large element of trust. It is in this respect that the standing of the Chief Executive in the eyes of his fellow Chief Executives is important, particularly in the counties. Personal characteristics play an important role in establishing meaningful and effective relationships.

There has been considerable debate on the size and the composition of a Chief Executives Department. The dangers of denuding the Chief Executive of any departmental responsibilities is that he can become a body without 'any eyes or ears'. It is for this reason that it is contended that the personnel function should report directly to him and that he should control and operate small departments providing a range of Management Services to the Authority.

There is a strong case in the metropolitan counties for a central planning group directly responsible to the Chief Executive; this need not be large, a small nucleus consisting of a very senior officer with a secretary and research assistant(s) would suffice. Such an officer would head the various working parties drawn from the specialists within the various departments, and from such bodies as the Transport Executive. Only in this way can a corporate plan be translated into action under someone who heads the Council's corporate management structure. In one case there has been resistance to this structure and it arises out of the old jealously guarded professional departmentalisms of traditional local government It may require a new generation of Chief Officers, bred into a corporate management concept to appear before these old practices can fade out!

When it comes to providing evidence of how Chief Executives perceive their role in
this office, a good guide is given by looking at their role within a council's
Safety Policy. In the two cases of which I have intimate knowledge, there are
differing approaches. The first sets out clear lines of authority and responsibility by stating:

"1. The Chief Executive

a. has overall responsibility etc. ....
b. will arrange for the implementation of the Council's Safety Policy
    and accordingly will support all persons carrying it out.

2. The Personnel Officer

a. will ensure that the Health and Safety Policy is reflected in an
    effective programme.

3. The Chief Officers

a. are accountable to the Chief Executive for compliance with all health
    and safety requirements by their staffs and by all contractors for
    which they are responsible.
b. shall take such steps as are required by the Chief Executive ...."

Contrast this with the Safety Policy of the second authority:

"The Chief Executive will be responsible for

1. Ensuring that there is a safety policy for the Council.

2. Ensuring that competent advice is avilable to management by
    appointing safety officers.

All Directors will be responsible for:

1. Ensuring that there is a written Safety Policy for their division,
    and the arrangements for dealing with them. The persons with
    special responsibilities in this matter will be named.

2. Ensuring that the Council's and Divisional Safety Policies are
    brought to the notice of all employees .... etc."

It will be noticed that the first policy defines the ultimate responsibility with
the Chief Executive, and that the other Chief Officers are accountable direct to
him. In the second it is vague and undefined. In the first, the Council's
Safety Officer can have his edict applied within the authority and with the backing
of the Chief Executive, while in the second, departmental independence is firmly
entrenched. When such a vital matter as safety, with its legal ramifications,
cannot be integrated into a corporate approach, there is little chance that it will
exist elsewhere in the authority. When the matter was raised with the Chief
Executive concerned, the answer was "I prefer to control activities such as this
by concensus and reserve positive direction for the relatively few instances where
it is necessary".

Areas of corporate management are not always clear to people within local government. One authority, faced with a financial crisis of alarming proportions,
decided on an "across the board" reduction of expenditure of ten per cent. This

seemed fair and gave a sense of equity, but it was not very long before building
maintenance was very seriously in difficulties. When there is a certain affluence
the fact that each department can spend sufficient money to maintain its buildings
is accepted; but when there is a serious backlog of omissions of work with leaking
roofs, rotting timbers, etc., there is a need to establish priorities for work.
This means that if Direct Works are employed as standard council policy, someone
has to make the decisions to allocate priorities. In larger institutions this
would fall on the Estates Department. Not so in most local authorities where each
department has sole 'ownership' rights. They may obtain and do, specialist advice
on the work needed, but at no time is there a single individual truly accountable
to the Council who can state the estimated outstanding repairs etc., and the effect
upon the buildings and the ultimate cost to the authority of postponing work
because of short-term economic tactical ploys.

This situation has raised the question of a corporate approach to estate management.
Councils are experienced in the management of housing estates. This calls for
specialist knowledge and experience, but the responsibility for the remainder of
the Council's estate is divided between various departments, and there is a need
for true estate management to be carried out. At best most estate departments of
councils are little more than municipal estate agencies, buying, leasing, and selling land! Only by a corporate approach to estate management can there be a single
person accountable to the Council members through the Chief Executive, although it
is not advocated that such a unit should be part of the Chief Executive's Department. If, however, Chief Executives could appreciate the full significance of
their role, then they would start to form a corporate structure within the
authority. It is probably true to say that you can determine the attitude of the
Chief Executive toward his corporate tole by the structure he has created to give
effect to it.

Which discipline is best suited for the post of Chief Executive

There has been considerable discussion in various Local Government and associated
journals on the appropriate discipline for the post of Chief Executive. In
private industry there was a period when either the lawyer or the accountant monop-
olised the managing director's chair. To-day in local government the same is true,
with very few exceptions. This argument means that each sees the whole operation
of the Council's work, either through various statutory duties and their legal
implications, or through financial control. Their emphasis on control mechanisms
tends to follow their own professional inclinations.

Regardless of professional discipline, the argument is never based on managerial
ability. There are those who contend that management was learned the hard way by
experience, and that they would never have got to the top but for some managerial
ability! This is not a particularly strong argument when in so many cases
professional ability has precedence over managerial considerations in many appointments to Chief Officer level. In the case of the Chief Executive it is the
corporate managerial ability which takes over from any consideration of professional ability. The subject of training within local government is dealt with later,
but this argument in favour of appointing either a lawyer or an accountant in
preference to any other skill provides further evidence that managerial skills are
seldom used as criteria in selection. In many cases little or no management training and development has taken place in the preparation for such a post, and even
for that matter for a departmental head.

Suffice it to say at this stage that there is a very strong case for having a firm
policy for management training throughout local government, enabling selection for
the most senior posts to be based more on managerial capability than professional
expertise. Once this is effected, the post of Chief Executive could be drawn from
any discipline.

The establishment of an organisational structure to implement the notion of
corporate management since 1974 has been through the establishment of such committees as the 'Management Team' or 'The Board of Managers'. The managerial content of
their activities, however, is very much open to question. It has been the practice
for Chief officers in presenting reports to various committees to outline policy
options and seldom to submit managerial implications of those options. While some
officers will strongly deny this, it is clear to any councillor who can appreciate
the difference. In consequence, the Management Team becomes in effect a body which
presents concensus policy options in those areas affecting more than one department.
There is in addition an unwritten law of 'Cabinet Collective Responsibility', in
that differing approaches by individual officers to that policy are never discussed
before elected members. These reports all deal with agreed policy, not agreed
managerial methods of implementation.

It must be borne in mind that local government expenditure is fundamentally about
priorities; whether there is a new primary school or a new elderly persons' home
or recreation centre, etc. Officers and members seldom see the choice in these
terms, as we shall see when we discuss the method of budgetting in Chapter 7.
There are resource implications resulting from policy options, but invariably these
are seen as additional staff or money, not the re-allocation of existing manpower
and finance! This is the basic gap in the decision making process when it comes to
policy determination. This explains the reason why chief officers find it convenient and easy at their board meetings to discuss policy matters rather than management problems.

Many chief officers will argue that their political masters expect this, since re-
allocation of resources, for example, means reducing services or activities on one
or more fronts when everyone accepts that the existing programme is the base for
expansion. Re-allocation mainly because of staff implication becomes unacceptable
politically. The inflexibility of resource management within local authorities
arises out of the total commitment by the two major parties to directly employed
staff of one kind or another, with the result that re-allocation of manpower brings
industrial problems for which local government is singularly ill-equipped to face,
and must imply either redundancies or an agreement which provides for major redeployment. Hence the unions are a party to this inflexibility of operation. The
whole conduct of affairs at this level suits the convenience of both politician
and officer. It makes for a quiet life. But it baulks change, particularly at a
time of severe financial restraint when priorities of choice assume a major item of
consideration.

The majority of the councillors find themselves trapped by this system in which a
large area of policy is predetermined by what could be described as an officers'
cabal, and which leaves them suspicious of officers' actions. There are very
serious implications in this situation which affect the councillors' position vis-
a-vis the public. This will be discussed in Chapter 6, but it reinforces the
analysis that the 'Management Team' concerns itself not with management problems
but policy statements. The outcry of protest at this statement is predictable.
When do committee chairmen, for instance, first get to grips with the policy
formation? I have never been a committee chairman, but I am a keen observer of
the manner in which they operate. They have every appearance from their conduct
and statements of giving the impression that they are fully briefed on the agreed
report - they never participate in its formation. In consequence they become the
political mouthpiece of the official line, whether it is based on a management
team report or on a departmental brief. This is not to say that politicians don't
lay down policy at times. They do. But often that policy is born of political
dogma without any feasibility study or management appraisal.

The officers naturally do their master's bidding, but the division between policy-
making and managerial implementation and control can at times be very sharp, while

at others it is blurred by the assumption of policy making roles by management
personnel. Policy making and management appraisal cannot take place in isolation
and it is the purist in organisational theory who while separating the roles fails
to organise their cohesion. There is a need for the policy makers and the management team to work together in establishing an acceptable policy and a programme for
implementation. Once or twice I have suggested for example that an elected member
should sit in on an officers' working party when investigating some aspect of
council operation. You should see the look of sheer horror on the faces of the
officers at such an outrageous suggestion. There is a school of thought, prevalent
in certain areas, and indicated by such public pronouncements as "this spreading
of information is due to an unfortunate requirement of the democratic process",
which sees elected members as a regrettable but necessary appendage to the local
government scene. Such officers see elected members and democracy as a threat to
their own empires. As a result the effective integration of the management team
with policy making is impossible.

If the management team is to be true to its title then there is a case for an inter-
locking structure with the policy makers. The crucial question is whether it is a
single party caucus, or a truly representative group of the elected members which
forms part of the real policy development process. There are, however, serious
dangers if it is left solely to a party caucus. There have been times when
important facts have, I gather, been revealed to a party's inner caucus, which if
revealed to the Council would have affected decisions. When this happens, it is
all too often that the unfortunate ratepayers are left to foot the bill. One such
instance occurred during a Council's financial crisis when the edict for a 10%
across the board cut was made as described earlier. I have every reason to believe
that the financial implication of this decision in the long term, with its
accelerated rotting of timbers and deterioration of roofs, was disclosed to at
least the Council Leader and possibly his inner caucus, but was withheld for one
reason or another from all other council members. The fact that councillors were
unaware of these implications and failed to query them is incidental to the process
whereby there can be concealment of vital facts due to the relationship between
members of the management team and a ruling party caucus. It must not be inferred
from the above that the management team should not discuss policy. There is a need
for a 'think tank' with supporting research services. This can only be done by the
officers in the absence of full-time paid councillors; in this capacity the
officers are the research group acting for and on behalf of the councillors. This
is substantially different from the pre-determined policy agreed by the officers
and subsequently presented to the council.

It is appropriate to ask at this stage why there is this lack of clarity on roles
as being managers and policy makers. One is basically historical, in that without
a clear management structure and with the professional independence referred to
earlier, management as such is a very neglected area of local government, and the
second is that very little has been done to implement management training areas
and to identify the corporate role. Training has not been totally neglected, but
the usual problems arise of training junior staff while senior staff assume
omnipotent management wisdom.

One of the clear gaps in local government organisation is the absence of a local
government staff college, or an acceptance that the administrative staff college
at Henley might be a suitable place for the concepts of corporate management to be
explained and studied through case study work. This will be discussed again in
Chapter 9. Since there is a maxim to which I have always held, namely "the
expectations of any organisation can never exceed those of the man with the
greatest power", this whole concept of corporate management which is implied in
appointing Chief Executives relies heavily on the corporate lead given by that
officer. Too often it has been a grandiose title and little else other than a
smoke screen for continuing where local government broke off in 1974.

CHAPTER 4

Staff Structure or "Your Guess is as Good as Mine"

It was inevitable that with re-organisation someone would have to devise a staff structure to enable the new authorities to operate from the 1st April 1974. With only a year from the election of the first councillor until the 1st. April 1974 when the authorities had to assume control, time was short for a thorough re-appraisal of staff requirements. Comparisons were therefore made with existing authorities which were virtually unchanged by re-organisation. In the case of the Metropolitan County Councils, the shire County Councils, many of which were little changed, provided a basis for assessment, while a few major cities like Manchester, which were virtually unchanged except for the transfer of a number of strategic matters to the Metropolitan County Councils, were the basis of Metropolitan District Council structure. The structures were therefore based upon existing knowledge rather than a re-think about the whole problem.

There was a general dearth of job descriptions in the former authorities, in consequence they were not readily available or even adaptable for use by the new councils. It was my privilege to serve on the Personnel Committee of the Greater Manchester Council and we took the opportunity to review the initial structure after two years. Yet there were new powers created for local government in the field of Consumer Protection which was broadened beyond the former trading standards tasks associated with the former County and County Boroughs by providing a consumer advice service. Although there was some pioneer work which had been done in London, yet there had to be some assessment of the potential work load before deciding on the appropriate structure of this department.

In the case of Highways a major policy decision had to be made on the matter of Agency Agreements, whereby some of the Highway functions could be carried out by the Metropolitan Districts on behalf of the County as the Highways Authority, with the cost incurred by the districts being re-imbursed by the Metropolitan County. This arrangement has naturally important implications for the staffing for both Councils. Further, once an agency agreement was operative it would be less easy to alter as it would require the transfer of staff between Authorities.

Greater Manchester has a wide ranging agency agreement which gave each District the task of designing schemes of under half a million pounds and carrying out other functions such as highway maintenance within predetermined financial limits. Once this decision was made, each tier of government was able to plan their staffing structure accordingly. However, neither the Highways or Personnel Committee

received any assessment of potential workload at the commencement of the agreement
in 1974, nor was an effective one produced at the review two years later. More
detail was supplied to me personally following my interrogation described later.
Previously there had been the Transportation Plan produced by SELNEC (South East
Lancashire & North East Cheshire). This included some four hundred schemes which
was estimated (in 1974 terms) to cost over half a million pounds each. But while
there was little or no indication of the likely money available, the anticipated
work load was guesswork for at this time the government was initiating yet another
method of arranging for transport programmes and their funding, known as the TPP
scheme (Transportation Policy and Programme), which is discussed in a later
chapter.

When the re-appraisal was carried out in 1976, the Personnel Committee had before
it the existing structure of the County Engineer's Department. In order that the
reader may understand the approach I took and the replies I received, the following
gives some indication. These points are extracted from my total submission of some
fifty-five major queries which included within them a number of supplementaries!

a) L.G.B. ".... there is an absence of job specification .... I am concerned
            about the level in the hierarchy of the department at which profess-
            al decisions and advice are given ...."

    C.E.   ".... job specifications have not been submitted" (no request was
            made for them) .... "job specifications are avilable for many posts in
            the department and work is proceeding on the remainder ...."

b) L.G.B. "I cannot believe that there are no copies of design work on the
            schemes handed over by the former Highways Authorities .... I cannot
            accept that all of the previous design work is unsuitable and has to
    C.E.   be re-designed ...."

    C.E.   ".... The content of preparation of the schemes varied from completely
            worked up schemes to schemes which simply consisted of single lines on
            a 1/2500 plan". The C.E. listed a number of schemes in the current
            transportation submission to the government, some had been reviewed
            and others were in the process of the review).

c) L.G.B. with reference to new design and construction division Highways
            planning group.
            "How are these teams deployed - what jobs?

    C.E.   "the information on the composition of the teams and the schemes on
            which they are working can be made available and if the committee
            require it will be produced for a subsequent meeting."

d) L.G.B. ".... I cannot accept the comment that there is a need for increased
            work on re-design" - was it so incompetent?

    C.E.   ".... There is no suggestion that the previous design work is incompet-
            ent; the instructions for the Transportation Strategy Joint Committee
            are quite clear; each scheme has to be reviewed in accordance with the
            current transportation policy with a view to blight being removed as
            quickly as possible."

Some idea will be gained from the above of the difficulties which a councillor
faces in coming to grips with the problem of agreeing a staffing structure. It is
extremely time consuming to go into detail if you are determined to be satisfied

that ratepayers' money is being wisely spent through the allocating of duties etc.,
to personnel. In the case of the Greater Manchester Council's 1976 review, the
papers setting out the assignment were available some ten days before the meetings,
but the scope of my questions, 53 for the County Engineers department and 30 for the
the County Planning officers, with their supplementaries built-in, meant that if
any meaningful discussion was to take place, these questions had to be forwarded in
sufficient time for the officer to provide me with the answers well before the
meeting, so that an effective oral examination of the points raised by the answers
could be carried out at the committee meeting.

The planning officer being the first of the two to be reviewed supplied his answers
at the meeting itself, which made it impossible for them not only to be studied
but for an effective cross-examination to take place. Having been caught out once
the County Engineer acceded to my request by sending his answers a few days in
advance.

The Personnel Committee was entrusted with the task of approving the assignments,
bearing in mind that there were strong hints that applications for additional posts
and the unfreezing of frozen posts was due to come before the following committee
meeting. There was no attempt by the officers to circulate my queries together
with their replies to other members of the committee other than the chairman and
vice-chairman. So what little discussion that was available was a dialogue in
which the other members of the committee were completely lost! But business being
what it is at these committees, when the chairman considers that it has proceeded
long enough, he imposes his own guillotine (Westminster is not the only place where
this occurs) and moves to the next business. He is supported of course by his
majority on the committee who feel faintly embarrassed by questions of a detailed
nature, but also by the officers who may be breathing down his neck in the hope of
relief! But so long as the committee has been seen to go through the process it
feels able to justify not only its approval of the officers' submissions but the
expense incurred in so doing!

To the casual reader all the effort may have seemed a useless exercise on my part.
However there is evidence that greater care was taken over future submissions
because no officer likes to feel himself under attack, and will take the necessary
steps. You do not win this round, but the task in the second is very much easier!

The assignment of posts in the planning department was scrutinised by me in a
similar fashion. There were three major sections: Structure Plan/Policy, Special
activities including joint reclamation, and Development Control/Local plans. There
were descriptions of the task for which the various sections were responsible, but
there were very general statements which did little to dispel my doubts concerning
various task assignments. The problem which a councillor faces in assessing the
validity of such submissions is indicated in one of the replies given to a
question.

"It is doubted whether in fact it is possible to represent the work of a planning
department by means of a series of organisation charts because of the nature of the
job and I have certainly never seen it done convincingly. In Greater Manchester
probably more than in the other areas, we have reached a degree of understanding
with the districts to avoid duplication and overlapping and have regular meetings
to ensure that there is no wasted effort".

The reader will decide for himself whether it would have been better to have
clearly defined tasks as between County and District, rather than "working lunches
etc." to avoid duplication etc., but the difficulty which ensues in establishing
the appropriate staff structure at both County and District becomes self-evident.
There is little doubt in my mind that the blurring of the edges of responsibility

can be a very convenient way of confusing councillors as to the exact location of the true accountability for actions.

One of the groups within the Planning Department was concerned with the preparation of the Structure Plan. Any layman would assume that once the Structure Plan was prepared, there could be some disestablishment of posts, or re-allocation to other areas where there was lower priority for completion during the preparation of the Structure Plan. Not so. Back came the answer:

"This is a misunderstanding of the Structure Plan process and the answer to this is really contained in paragraph 15 of the introductory report. It has been made quite clear by Government that regional structure planning is a continual process and that the work does not stop or pause at any particular submission."

Not even one post was to be disestablished or redeployed. It is tantamount to accepting an argument that once a building has been completed, the work force should be retained at full strength to retain it! I never received an answer to my satisfaction that there was any justification for the projected retention after completion of the Structure Plan of all those within the section who were originally assigned to its preparation. This was not the only area where staff were assigned to a task which had apparently limited duration. There was a group under the County Engineer in his capacity of Engineer to the Airport responsible for designing the second runway. Bearing in mind the delays in starting the runway, let alone its final abandonment for a limited extension of the existing runway, there are no plans, I gather, for redeployment of staff at a later date.

If there is one point which must be brought to the attention of all councillors serving on Personnel or Establishments Committees, it is that once a post is established and filled for whatever purpose, it is the devil's own job to disestablish it. Councillors should be most wary indeed of those posts designed for a task which is seen to be of limited duration. It is one of the well established devices whereby officers persuade councillors to increase their total staff, justifying the immediate appointment by reference to a high priority task. Very few officers are prepared to reduce the degree of priority of one or more schemes with its consequential redeployment of personnel.

Bearing in mind the cut-back in Highway schemes in recent years, there appears to have been very little reduction in staff from the time that it was all go! But the councillor must beware of the automatic answer to this question. The reply inevitably will be that we must plan, i.e. design, road schemes ready for the off! Hence of course we get back to the situation where there are 400 odd schemes in various stages which incidentally at 1974 rates of construction would have taken over one hundred years to build! This problem of usage of design staff is discussed in the chapter on Project Planning.

The difficulty facing a councillor in trying to solve staffing and allocation of duties is seen by a battle in which I was engaged over the Traffic Management Unit. This unit deals amongst other things with the assessment of the highway problems likely to arise if planning permissions are granted by the districts. At the time of the 1976 review, information was given that some 10,000 applications a year had a highway content. Of these 10,000 applications which are examined by the County's Divisional Engineers located at the District Councils, some 1600 are referred by the Divisional Engineers to County Hall for advice and processing, in addition to some 2,000 relevant to the Manchester District, where there is no Divisional Engineer. An examination of the salary grades in relation to the posts reveals that the Divisional Engineers were appointed on grade PO3. The Traffic Management Unit at County Hall is headed by an officer on grade PO5, with assistants for various functions on PO3. If therefore the Divisional Engineer on PO3 has not the authority to make the decision himself but must refer them to County Hall, it would be a reasonable assumption that someone better qualified and on a higher grade would make the various decisions. Therefore the head of the group on PO5 is the only person who measures up to this assumption (if salary is commensurate with qualifications and experience!) Looking at the position of the head of this group, there are nine districts (excluding Manchester) each of which on average copes with some 1,100 applications of which approximately 176 are referred to County Hall, totalling 1,600. Leaving aside the Manchester District applications, this work load is 500 in excess of that dealt with by each Divisional Engineer! Of course the Divisional Engineer has other tasks to do, but so has the Head of the Traffic Management Unit, who has responsibility for implementing traffic management schemes, besides undertaking special projects such as (at the time of writing) a proposed accident unit!

There is only one solution if such a work load is ever to be dealt with satisfact-orily. It is that someone other than the Head of the group within the headquarters based staff has to make the decision, i.e. someone on PO3 grade or below. My con-tention was, 'don't you trust your Divisional Engineer?' I never had a satisfact-ory answer to this point, but it reinforced an opinion which I have always felt about a headquarters staff and area management schemes of this nature. It is that there is a notion that if decisions are made at County Hall they must be right (even if made by someone lower in the hierarchy), and it is the ones made "away from the eagle eye of the Chief" at Divisional level that are suspect!

This whole subject raises the question of the level of professional competence within various posts. There appears to be an abhorence in delegating professional decisions. Every committee report goes out under the name of the appropriate Chief Officer, yet the officer who prepares the report very rarely faces the committee himself, and if someone at an outpost prepared it, it would be called in and re-drafted! I have always contended that professionally qualified personnel sould be empowered to make decisions on professional matters (within the determined overall policy of the council) according to their qualifications and experience. Further, the high salary many are paid must be a reflection of the responsibility to make professional decisions. I have publicly challenged a Chief Officer on this point, but have been rebuffed! The failure to permit the execution of professional responsibility can lead to a top heavy organisation with its consequential frus-trations of many junior staff and a general lowering of the morale. This situation justifies the criticism of overstaffing of local government. For every member of staff who has to process paper without making any decisions adds to the bureau-cracy and the ratepayers' burden.

Whenever a councillor challenges the staffing structure, the perennial defence by the officers is to obtain a table of comparability with other organisations. When such tables are presented, no clear explanation is given which would explain the difference in staffing levels if they are unfavourable to the reviewing authority. There is considerable difficulty in making true and effective comparison between even similar type of authorities, particularly here in the case of Highways, different Metropolitan Counties operate various types of Agency Agreements with their districts. However in order to justify the G.M.C.'s staffing in 1976 levels the following is an extract of the table of comparison presented to the Personnel Committee.

Table of Highways Staff

	G.M.C.	West Midlands	Merseyside	South Yorkshire	Tyne & Wear
Population	2729900	2785400	1620750	1319180	1198390
District Councils	10	7	5	4	5
Chief officer	1	1	1	1	1
Deputy	–	1	1	1	–
Special Salary Grade	6	15	6	22	14
P.O. Grades	94	117	63	114	41
Department Total Posts	625	514	261	435	345
Total Cost	£ 2145399	2109687	1016838	2021636	1273087

In addition to the different agency agreements referred to there were different organisation practices, the G.M.C. undertook the school crossing patrol service which in other authorities is undertaken by the police. In some authorities the accountancy function in respect of highways was centralised within the Treasurers Department. There were other differences. One feature revealed by the table shows clearly this ratio of 'Chiefs to Indians'. Taking P.O. Grades and above as chiefs, the proportion of the total posts that such a group represents reads as follows for each respective Metropolitan County.

18%	27%	29%	33%	18%

The average salary of all posts within the various departments was given as

£3433	£4104	£3895	£4647	£3690

Clearly the G.M.C. and Tyne and Wear appear less top heavy than the other authorities but there must be very serious doubts about the staffing structure in South Yorkshire, although this county did not have an agency agreement with its four districts. Even so it does not explain the top heavy nature of the organisation. Faced with this information the reader will be able to glean the sense of self-congratulation felt by many of the G.M.C.'s Personnel Committee that they had got things right and with self-justification abandoned discussion of the crucial points of their own organisation which I had raised!

One officer when faced with my questionnaire stated that there was no difficulty in answering eighty per cent of the questions, it was the twenty per cent which were difficult. How vital it is, therefore, that the twenty per cent should be identified and above all eventually either justified or disestablished? If it was difficult to explain away the twenty per cent in the Greater Manchester Council, how great was the percentage in other authorities?

In view of the re-organised structure of local government it would have been very useful to have had comparative studies of the staff pre-and post-April 1974 of all local government outside London. It would also be useful if the total highways staff could be compared. It certainly was never done within the G.M.C. conurbation. It would have enabled an assessment of whether there was an expansion or contraction of public servants following April 1974. Were the new authorities streamlined?

Or was it as far as staff was concerned, a redeployment exercise?

There is a generally accepted practice that staff assignments are submitted to the appropriate Service Committee before being passed on to the Personnel Committee. The Service Committees however seldom spend any time examining the submissions in any detail, being guided by the departmental head to leave such a scrutiny to the Personnel Committee. Each committee has a natural wish to expand its activity. This satisfies a covert sense of power associated with a desire to be seen to be contributing to the well-being of others, and to the general effectiveness of the authority. The Service Committee therefore sees itself as guardian for their Chief Officer and feels duty bound to support him in matters of increased staffing. Personnel Committee feels under no such obligation and casts itself in the role of being a devil's advocate, denying additional staff whenever possible. It could be argued that this is a healthy check. However, due to the fact that some members of the Personnel Committee also serve on the Service Committee, it is not surprising to find members change their stance as frequently as they change their "committee hat".

The Greater Manchester Council had a practice of inviting the Chairman and Vice-Chairman of the Service Committee concerned to attend, to answer the Personnel Committee's queries and to justify any proposal to release frozen posts or to establish additional posts. This practice is the exception as far as most authorities of which I am aware. The presence of the Chairman is of little value unless he is fully conversant with the very considerable detail of the department's operation, yet it is healthy for him to come under interrogation in the event of possible later discussion at a full council meeting. His contribution, however, is very secondary to that of the officer concerned and helps to keep the Chairman on his toes as being the person who is ultimately accountable to the electorate. Although some officers could find the presence of the Chairman a convenient screen!

When investigation into staffing levels are undertaken, the role of the Personnel Officer will depend upon his position within an authority. Sometimes there is a centralised Personnel section which processes all proposed changes, while in other cases he may be may be an adviser called in at the whim of the departmental chief. Where the latter situation arises, it adds further evidence of an authority's lack of appreciation of the corporate approach, but worse still it indicates that the Chief Executive has little or no effective control over manpower resources deployment, which must hinder him in the task of controlling the authority's activities. If the application is processed through the Personnel Officer, he will naturally defend the submission. In such a case the councillor has to have confidence in the Personnel Officer's professional integrity and competence, which has to be earned; it cannot be taken for granted. This necessitates the Councillor being willing to see for himself outside the committee meeting that the appropriate questions are being asked and the correct answers given.

There is little evidence, when staff assignments have been agreed, of any follow-up to ensure that these assignments are filled in accordance with the approved submission. I discovered as a result of talking to staff that six additional posts, assigned on the basis that it was necessary to have at least two persons on each refuse tip in order that one should be available in the event of an accident, and so safeguard the authority under the Health & Safety at Work Act, were not all posted to the tips specified, but they were used only to supplement staffing levels at other tips. Some of those tips specified as being in need of additional personnel remained one-man operated, thus nullifying reasons put forward to increase the establishment. So in spite of specific tasks being assigned and approved by the Committee and the Council, some officers can be found to have circumvented the decisions of the elected members, some of whom when the matter is raised turn a blind eye, it seems, to such courses of action. I personally have raised this

whole question, but never during one of my terms of office did I receive a satisfactory answer. It must be remembered that sometimes it is very convenient for
officers to indulge in procrastination as election time approaches, and so gamble
on the electoral system curtailing a member's opportunity to continually scrutinise
their actions and activities. This is particularly important in the case of County
elections where the whole council is elected at one time. The post-election
settling-in period, if there are major changes, provides the officers with a ready-
made smokescreen.

At the time of their creation in 1974, some authorities decided not to make all
the appointments to a planned establishment, but to leave certain appointments
unfilled till later when the organisation had settled down. This was a very
reasonable approach, provided that there was a thorough appraisal undertaken at the
time when the request to fill any of the "vacancies" was made. If these unfilled
posts were found to be superfluous after a specific period, they were disestablished in some instances. This was the exception and subsequently became a device
whereby the Chief Officer sought to trade this particular unfilled post for a new
one It was essential for a councillor to be alert to this possible subtle device
to help convince him that this action was correct. Further justification often
arose when the two appropriate salary grades overlapped and the replacement post
started on a lower increment, so effecting a paper saving since there was as yet
no cost incurred due to the unfilled post.

This is not the only time that positions on the salary scale with its innumerable
increments are used as a device to convince members of the wisdom of the proposals.
In times of financial cut-backs any proposal which can be shown to effect a saving
has an automatic headstart. I have seldom known any re-organisation proposal not
endeavour to demonstrate a saving by using the position on the salary scale as a
device for so doing. It is only when the appointees have advanced along these
salary scales or even applied for a re-grading, that the true cost of the proposal
can be calculated!

It is noticeable that the unfilled posts were often nearer to the bottom of the
hierarchy rather than the top. This is a fairly common experience. Investigation
will show that the undermanning of the Police Force for instance did not affect
the number of sergeants, superintendents, etc. The vacancies are concentrated at
the rank of constable.

It should not be forgotten that organisational structure has a profound effect upon
the salary structure. The salary of the Chief Executive is basically geared to
the rateable value of the authority on the basis that rateable value reflects in
some measure the coverage of responsibility. It has considerable validity. The
departmental Chief Officers have their salaries proportional to that of the Chief
Executive. Taking two areas of Highways and Planning, the justification for
County Officers having higher salaried posts in this field is self-evident when
you compare the responsibilities of those within the County's constituent districts.

However, there are cases where the responsibilities are not comparable. Take the
Personnel function as an example. The responsibility is proportional to the
number of employees and not to rateable value. Should the Chief Personnel Officer
of the County authority be designated a Chief Officer, he would qualify for a
salary proportional to the Chief Executive; such a payment will be out of all proportion to that paid to a similar post in the Districts, where they could have up to
four times the number of employees of those employed by the County.

This form of anomaly by the historical development of organisation structure is
very unsatisfactory, and provides evidence that in many cases salaries and responsibilities do not go hand in hand. This becomes more glaring when a close study

of delegation takes place. Some departments have developed a high degree of
delegation, others have little, yet the salary scales operative within an authority
are determined in large measure by the comparison with similar posts and the so-
called going rate, rather than any defined delegated responsibilities attached to
the posts. Such a step could lead to job evaluation, which is a subject which
makes all officials of the National and Local Government Officers (N.A.L.G.O.)
squirm in their offices.

The unions are very experienced in national negotiations and most of their individual officers have very many years' experience behind them. The employers' side,
consisting sometimes of a mixture of officers and members, has not the breadth of
experience. When negotiations centre round technical (if that is the right term?)
services, this lack of experience can be a very serious handicap indeed. Of
course, the employers' side have their own professional staff to guide them, but
where there are so many technical services involved, the knowledge of how these
services operate in the field is sometimes very sparse compared with that of the
union representatives. As a result, the unions are able to run rings round the
employing authorities at the ratepayers' expense!

This is very clear from the state of negotiations early in 1979 when the employers
made an offer in response to the social workers' claim. There were a number of
issues involved, but the crucial part of the offer dealing with salary grades was
the basis upon which the former three grades of welfare assistant, unqualified
social worker and qualified social worker, were to be revised into five grades,
two covering welfare assistants and three for social workers. It may have been
incidental that the top salary of the social worker would have been increased by
£1000 at a time of 5% pay norms!! The crux of the offer changed the whole method
of operation of local authority social services. Where salaries were based upon
experience and qualification, the proposal changed it to one based upon the degree
of difficulty of the casework undertaken. To explain this further, it will be
appreciated that the degree of complexity of a particular case is not always known
at the time of the initial contact. Was it therefore the intention of the employers
to shift a case from one social worker to a more senior, and onwards as the case
became more complex? If so, it runs counter to the current modus operandi that it
is better to keep a single contact between a worker and his client. The role of a
highly qualified social worker was to provide the necessary back-up service and
advice. Only in special cases would there be a transfer of a case from one worker
to another.

If the employers' proposal is accepted and agreed, it will become a charter for the
unions to upgrade a substantial number of social workers, whatever their initial
grade.

It was inevitable that reorganisation into larger authorities would provide a very
different approach in the task of managing staff. The effect of this on management
was twofold. Firstly, reorganisation transferred from the smaller authorities to
the new larger units officers who had limited experience in the task of handling
large numbers of directly employed persons. Secondly, even the former large authorities did not attract to the ranks of their staff commercially minded people.
One of the reasons for the creation of municipal undertakings was to avoid some
aspects of commercialism which were considered to be undesirable. It must be
stressed that the former separate municipal undertakings of Gas and Electricity
disappeared from local government control with the advent of nationalisation in
the late '40s, although Water remained municipalised until reorganisation in 1974.

Local authorities considered that it could improve industrial relations by having
joint consultation, yet local government doesn't understand the difference between
negotiation and consultation. There are within local government numerous Joint

Committees for various grades and occupations which are termed consultative, when they are in reality negotiating bodies. They are concerned with negotiating aspects of terms and conditions of service. In drawing attention to this slovenly use of the words consultation and negotiation, which is endemic in organisations unable to grasp the practicalities of industrial life, I am not decrying the establishment of committees to undertake negotiation. Once the difference between negotiation and consultation is appreciated, it might be possible to get down to the real problem of implementing consultation, and to the means whereby management may effectively implement council policy through its employees.

Consultation should achieve two fundamental purposes. The first is to identify the framework within which management is free to manage, and the second to enable the knowledge and experience of employees being made available to assist management in the achievement of its objectives. The first aim is to avoid industrial action, or at least to identify those areas where there is a possibility of industrial action. Unless management is aware of these limits, beyond which there is a possibility of action by its employees, it will act in the dark. It is possible, however, that the communication process involved to give effect to consultation on management's policy may be able to extend the limits within which management can manage, due to increased understanding of the issues and problems involved. Consultation, if effectively operated, must result in improved communications.

The refuse collection dispute which occurred in Stockport in 1978 resulted mainly from policy decisions being made without a thorough exploration of the managerial implications, and more especially without a thorough consultation on the manner in which the various options could be implemented. This process must not be construed as one where there is management by committee, or the 'tail wags the dog'. The dispute was evidence of a lack of effective consultation and communication.

There is another aspect of consultation which should be explained. Consultation does not require equality of representation of management and employee. It is important that all levels of employees (this includes staff) should be represented and that it is conducted by the manager responsible for the matter under consultation. The manager can delegate this task. Negotiation on the other hand requires equal representation of management and employee groups concerned.

If therefore management within local government could discern the difference, considerable progress could be possible in making local government more efficient and effective.

CHAPTER 5

The Role of a Councillor or "Cultivate a Mushroom"

A person's personality has an important influence in determining the possible success in a post. It is particularly true of councillors. The attributes which make up a good councillor depend upon the perspective of the viewer. Some constituents assess the value of their councillor according to the number of thorns he or she sticks into the side of the officers, while those councillors liked by officers may be completely unresponsive to their electorate's wishes. There is always a danger that long service may cause the councillor to drift from the first type to the second when he or she allows their critical faculties to become blunted with familiarity and friendship.

The two major parties view the concept of 'Community Politics' with contempt, yet its birth derives from the gap between the man-in-the-street and his councillor, which is fostered by the abundance of professional expertise being used to ensure that the lay councillor becomes putty in the hands of the officer. The statement by a very senior officer in which he derided the necessity to engage in consultation with those affected by a scheme put forward by his department is indicative that officers too can become insensitive to the effect of certain proposals upon individuals, with the result that the officer himself can become part of the wedge opening up the gap between the ratepayer and the council. Such an officer sees himself as the culmination of acquired knowledge, and the layman as an unnecessary appendage who is a potential threat to the exercise of his professionalism.

The growth of local government and its powers within society has created a feeling of elation among the officers who consider that nothing is gained from going outside its service to learn new techniques and skills. Private industry is seen as a 'painted lady', undermining the position of the State as it functions through and by a local authority. Yet the pressure of commercial viability does create change and innovation, but local authorities, by and large, existing without those pressures are so slow to adopt new techniques and, above all, modern management practices, they have therefore developed their own brand of inertia, cocooned from the realities of life. Many assume universities to be ivory towers, yet local authorities are so cloistered that any employee seeking to break out of their bondage has precious little chance of being accepted by private enterprise.

It is against this background that most councillors have to function. The majority have to operate within a system alien to their normal working life. Those councillors who are employed in the public sector often have a 'companionship of interest' that blunts their perception and assists in establishing this gap between

the elector and the elected member; for, after all, such a system is the one they
know best and in which they feel at home.

It is unsatisfactory to consider the role of the Councillor without understanding
the process of their election. Those who are members of either of the two major
parties are by and large elected as a result of public reaction to national
politics. Those of other parties together with the independents tend to be elected
as a result of known public service or commitment which overcomes national issues.
In consequence there are proportionately more councillors committed to providing a
local service regardless of national party dogma amongst the latter group. This is
not to say that there are not some very devoted local activists in either the
Labour or the Conservative parties; there are. Yet it is not unknown for a member
to be elected due to the 'colour of his or her ribbon'. After the Conservative
landslide in the County elections in 1977, there were reports of some elected
persons being unwilling initially to sign their declaration of acceptance of office
because they allowed their name to go on the nomination sheet in sufferance, so
that at least the seat was fought! Such is the effect of party colours and the
desire of the electorate to express a view of national politics through local
elections. Members elected in this way are often at a loss to discern their per-
ceived role, while the others see it as undertaking the duties of a local ombudsman!

The party system operated within local government means that policy making is confined to an elite within the majority party, to the exclusion of other councillors.
There are many matters where there is little or no party political issue at stake,
but in spite of this some of the ablest councillors are excluded from this inner
circle. Even within the majority party, commitments to place of employment sometimes severely curtails the time available for undertaking committee chairmanships.

Leaders of Councils will strenuously deny the exclusion of minority parties claiming
that most Policy Committees have their membership drawn from all shades of political opinion. But to believe that the major items of policy are effectively discussed at that committee is very naive, because it ignores the power and influence of
the party whip wielded by the ruling party caucus. It is known that a number of
councillors within the Tory party caucus do favour the concept of benevolent
dictatorship (to describe it in moderate terms) and that they have been known to
voice this view openly to officers. The real debate on policy-making, therefore,
takes place outside the public meeting and behind closed doors where even professional advice is excluded. This is more common where the ruling party has a substantial majority. Anyone who has studied the 'in-fighting' within the majority
group of the Greater Manchester Council since the 1977 election on such subjects
as Consumer Protection, the proposed National Ice Skating Rink, the Major Theatre,
to mention only a few, will find sufficient evidence to confirm this statement
that in spite of strongly held differences, within the party they present in
committee a public facade of unanimity.

The influence of the parliamentary party upon local party politics cannot be dis-
counted, whether the particular party is in opposition or in government. An
illustration of this type of influence occurred when the dictum of the then
Secretary of State to the Regional Health Authoritys' Chairman laid down that the
Board members being appointees of the Secretary of State are bound to do the
Minister's bidding!! If they don't, they should resign! While this instance
occurred outside local government, it demonstrates that Government ministers can
wield influence to counter local independence. Similarly, the dictat of the Tory
Parliamentary spokesman to his members of the County Councils over the establish-
ment of consumer protection services can have a similar effect to that which
occurred with the Health authority, even though the party is in opposition at
Westminster and without the sanctions available to the party in government.
Adherence to such edicts arises sometimes out of personal aspirations to be

favourably considered for appointment to 'Quangos' once a change in government
takes place, or even to possible endorsement for selection as a prospective parliamentary candidate. The influence of national party leaders upon the actions or
inactions of their local councillors in the case of the two major parties cannot
be underestimated. It can destroy local independence but it does show power of
patronage!

Those involved in local politics frequently have to face the electors who challenge
the need for the pettiness of party politics in local government. Many council
candidates have considerable sympathy for this view. If any elected member really
analyses the issues with which he is faced, he will find it almost unnecessary to
have party politics except for a very limited number of fundamental issues. Most
of local government is about implementation of policies which, if adequately
discussed, find substantial common ground for implementation. There are, however,
certain pressures which made it convenient for certain councillors to play the
party political game.

The first is the use of full council to give a public airing of national politics.
I have found one major party on one council take up an inordinate amount of
council time debating their national policy issues, like the operation of Housing
Associations, without any relevance to their operation as it affects the Council's
own conduct of affairs. While it might be appropriate to criticise the Chair for
permitting such debates, the abuse of the public platform of Council meetings is
an established practice which does the cause of local government little good.

The second is the control of members through the party whip. This makes the prediction of the result of the debates a foregone conclusion. It is extremely
convenient to both the party caucus and to many officers. The use of the party
whip is so important a facet in the life of the councillor that it is discussed in
the next chapter.

The third is the see-saw of politics. The cycle of change (in some areas shorter
than others) provides a chance for political power to rotate. Without the party
system the chances for many councillors to become chairmen or vice-chairmen of
committees or to serve on outside bodies would diminish. Accordingly, party
politics provides the convenience of 'Buggin's turn'. This is in sharp contrast
to the position as it existed in the former rural and urban districts, where such
posts were shared between parties with the most able of the councillors being
appointed without subservience to a party caucus. Those who decry the former days
should reflect on what has been destroyed by reorganisation! Most councillors
have a streak of vanity within them, some more overt than others; the party system
gives a suitable outlet when on seeking re-election a list of committee membership
and membership of numerous other bodies can be presented to delude the electorate
as to the contribution, let alone its quality!

I remember seeing one candidate's list of the organisations to which he belonged.
It almost read like a trade directory!

Involvement of Councillors

Chapter 9 deals with management and discusses the organisational structure.
Reference is made there to the possible interplay between the committee structure
and the organisation structure. In the past it was very common to have a
committee to oversee a department, rather than a function which involved a number
of departments. This is the hereditary basis for the departmentalism so
prevalent even to-day.

The duty of the elected member on a committee is seen as overseeing the department's function, with the chairman of the committee acting as the political spokesman of the Chief Officer. In some cases the identification of the committee member with the department is itself so strong that he or she can become an arch-advocate regardless of the weight of criticism levelled at the conduct of affairs. This occurred even in the former smaller authorities where the party whip was less in evidence. In other cases, the committee view, however strong, can be trampled on by the party caucus without even public discussion. Most decisions and policy 'u-turns' are taken behind closed doors'.

The factors which determine the committee structure in spite of the Bains report are still influenced in the case of the metropolitan county councils by the need to find something for the councillors to do. This may seem strange, but it was one of the factors which determined the Greater Manchester Council's committee structure in the early days. It was hoped to provide every member with at least two committees which would provide enough job satisfaction and involvement without causing trouble to the party caucus. This affected the majority party in particular. The other factors were the maximum numbers suitable for committee work in relation to the total number of councillors. It is, therefore, perfectly feasible for the number of committees to be determined by such arithmetical calculation, rather than a relationship to desirable functional activities of the council. This criticism is less true of the metropolitan districts than it is of the metropolitan counties.

Every councillor wishes to get involved in council work and the decision-making process. In a metropolitan district a backbencher can expect to serve on two major committees out of the eight or so that exist. There are often several sub-committees dealing with various aspects; they usually have a more limited membership, although this is not always the case. The task of dealing effectively, as a back-bencher, with these two major committees can be difficult, especially when there is a long cycle of meetings which can be of two months' duration. It is not unknown for a councillor to receive some seventy pages on a single subject, such as staff proposals, which arrive on a Friday morning before a meeting on the following Monday evening. Yet that document is only one of many to be discussed at that meeting. How can a member really get to grips with the issues? It is even worse in the planning field where officers, having spent months preparing documents such as a draft area plan or even a draft county structure plan for a whole county, then present the full report to a committee for comment or approval. Little wonder that contributions are negligible from many members. However much the officers try to feed-in basic documents over a period of time to keep elected members informed of developments, it is not always easy for the members to retain the gist of previous reports, when the same councillor has a multitude of other matters for consideration, not to mention various activities and events he or she is expected to be involved in. Councillors are expected to keep up-to-date by their constit-uents, yet the officers have the advantage over them of a more closely defined activity.

It is pertinent at this stage to comment that some officers do express a desire to see elected members taking an effective part in policy formation. There is always the danger, however, that should councillors become so overwhelmed by paper, together with the pressures of their employment, that they may be unable to devote sufficient time to absorb the full import of the documents. The officers may then become disheartened and, worst of all, sceptical of the elected members' contribut-ion. In such cases there is always the possibility that the independence of officers from elected member involvement increases to the detriment of the Council's operation.

This raises very important issues which are not easy to solve. How far can and are members able to associate themselves with the process of policy evolvement? Clearly there is a need for members to be involved more closely with the work of

the various departments. The separate deliberation of the officers and the members
can only continue to perpetuate the divide, especially when party cauci meet to
determine policy without officer involvement. (I should stress that I do not
believe that officers should attend such meetings). It is, however, abundantly
clear that members should be involved in various working parties considering
aspects of policy, and that such membership should not be confined to chairmen,
vice-chairmen or members of the majority party. The reaction of certain officers
to the suggestion that a member who was undertaking a performance review on the
problems of security should attend a working party indicates not only the alarm at
the departure from tradition, but almost a sense of insecurity on the part of the
officers that members may actually see what is being done! It also indicates the
potential opposition of some officers to a greater interplay between member and
officer in the working of the council's affairs. Such an attitude in my view
leaves too much to be desired.

Some authorities do have elected members attending the meetings of the Management
Board. Since some members have considerable managerial experience it might be
possible to ensure that the preoccupation with trivia (sometimes a reported feature
of these board meetings!) might be avoided and an effective management control and
reporting system established. In addition, if in preparing the policy options,
elected members attended the working parties it would enable them to make effective
contributions in the council's debates based on first hand knowledge of the issues
(rather than garbled reported statements).;

The recent action (January 1979) of the tanker drivers' dispute which had the
effect of closing a vast number of schools demonstrated in many instances a complete
lack of contingency planning, with the inevitable result that leading members of
the council had to take emergency action without the benefit of any well thought
out contingency plans. If officers are unable to do their management task of
forward thinking, particularly when industrial action of one kind or another is the
order of the day, it becomes grossly unfair if they present the policy makers with
emergency situations with inadequate preparation. The task of members remains that
of instructing the officers to get on and do their job properly, for after the
tanker drivers is anyone to suggest that other groups might not disrupt the
provisions of the public service?

To those who would argue that officers are able to speak at the committee meetings
(although not voting), it should be emphasised that it is the established practice
in many authorities for the various departments to be represented at such meetings
by the Head of the Department (and sometimes Section Heads). Frequently the
officer who has done the basic work is not present, his identity is not even revealed in the documents, and often the 'official spokesman' has not been fully briefed.
I have had personal experience of situations due to discussions with junior officers
on particular aspects when this has arisen, and also where statements made at one
sub-committee by a junior officer have been totally ignored and twisted by a more
senior officer to give a completely different slant. Councillors need to explore
more deeply some of the issues in spite of the alarm felt by some officers at the
prospect that members might gain inside knowledge! Councillors should be alerted
to the need to detect whether such a reaction is due to ignorance of the facts, or
to a 'Watergate' operation. I was once accused of knowing more than the Chief
Executive!

Councillors should always be alert to the danger of being hoodwinked. Some traditionally minded councillors will be appalled at such an intrusion into departmental
operations. Some of them will be those who simply attend meetings, rather than
contribute to the Council's deliberations. I have always found that informed
opinion is always listened to regardless of the party. All who serve as councillors
should ponder on this. It may well be that the political game would produce a

'paper' defeat, by this I mean that if the information runs counter to the declared
action or policy of the ruling party, the formal vote - if on a motion - will be
defeated, but great care will be taken to investigate and to effect changes if the
information is substantiated and can bring criticism to the Council through references to the District Auditor or Ombudsman. It has often been my own experience
that I have been heavily defeated on a motion where I have been critical of the
officers' proposals or management's operation, yet afterwards action has been taken
to prevent a repeat performance. It is useful for some councillors, especially
those in opposition to the ruling party to remember that 'you don't always have to
win in order to succeed.'

Before leaving the topic of member involvement, attention should be drawn to the
position arising when policy and industrial relations intertwine. There can easily
be a chicken and egg situation where a policy may be decided before management's
negotiation with employees takes place. In such a case the employees, knowing the
policy decision, may put a price upon its implementation; equally, a predetermined
agreement with the unions could rule out an alternative policy option. The
Stockport Council's problem over the refuse collection system is a classical
example of a situation where a particular policy option was decided by militancy
among a clique of employees who were determined to run matters their own way.

The preferred option was based on a scheme which provided (at least on paper) substantial savings. The scheme met with substantial resistance from the residents so
the Council had to go back to the original list of options and chose the second
best, but which overcame most of the criticisms made of the preferred scheme.
Having made the decision, certain sections of the workforce still took industrial
action, and consequently when it was finally settled there was a price for settle-
ment extracted out of the authority. There was never a report to the Council of
the eventual financial outcome of the new scheme. Bearing in mind that the change
in collection methods was made to curtail council expenditure, it is possible that
the time and effort (never calculated) of the officers and others working to
provide a final acceptable solution and an agreement with the refuse collectors
may have in the end effected very minimal costs.

There are important lessons to be learned, but whether they will be heeded is
doubtful. It is clear that in a number of instances the choice of a particular
option necessitates negotiations with the Unions, but it is important that the
Council's choice and the union consent to the revised working arrangement should
not pre-empt either the one or the other. Further, it is thoroughly unsatisfactory
to choose an option when the eventual financial outcome is extremely speculative or
even unknown. The choice of option and the agreement may in a number of instances
have to proceed in tandem. It is quite unacceptable for the policy-makers not to
be involved in the actual negotiation process. It requires a joint member and
officer team and those who are the elected representatives should be drawn from all
shades of opinion. It should not be beyond the wit of those in local government
to devise the mechanism for this.

The suggestion for joint member and officer involvement in policy development and
negotiation is not made without an awareness that it calls for an even greater
commitment in terms of time than at present. However, it might make many committee
meetings more meaningful, besides allowing the public to hear informed discussion
rather than the 'reading through' process which occurs so often. Whether such a
proposal will call for salaried councillors is discussed in the final chapter, but
I am sure that many thinking people would be horrified at the procedure in many
authorities to-day, and would want and expect their councillors to perform better.

A discussion of the role of the councillors must include some comment upon the
tactics used in politics. Sometimes politicians grossly mislead the public to

arouse support for their candidature. It is probably one of the least desirable
and honest actions by those who hold positions of leadership and trust as public
figures. Most of us who are engaged in politics may have committed such indiscret-
ions purposely or inadvertently, but it is an action, once the hoax has been
rumbled, which can only leave the general public with a very jaundiced view of
public figures.

I take as an example a suggestion made when Manchester Airport decided to extend
their runway instead of building a second runway as originally proposed some two
years previously. Whichever course the airport authority took, there would still
have been a political clamour, not confined to one party, for the lorries carrying
the stone from the Derbyshire Peak District to be conveyed by rail. Firstly,
there is no rail line into the airport, so either one would have to be built which
would be valuable if it be put to permanent use after completing the works, such as
passenger traffic, or the nearest suitable siding would have to be adapted.
Secondly, the suggestion by politicians that the quarries in Derbyshire are on the
rail was misleading. There are a number on the rail, but those which are, form
part of a long production process which has been going on over the years, and has
therefore absorbed the capital costs of rail transfer. One such quarry which uses
surplus stone, manufactures cement, but conveys that cement not by rail but by
bulk tank carriers on the roads. Most of the quarries supplying the construction
industry are away from rail connections and it would be almost impossible to
connect all possible quarries with a rail link.

Thirdly, if such a proposal for rail transport was enforced there would be a
requirement to build a suitable plant for transferring the stone from the rail
wagons and tipping it into lorries at the terminal near the airport end. But there
would have to be one or more such plants at the nearest appropriate rail access,
depending upon the location of quarries used. Bearing in mind the capital costs of
such works, it could amount to an additional 20% of the cost of the stone. Such
possible costs are never discussed in any political propaganda. Fourthly, there
appears not to have been any inquiry into the availability of suitable wagons by
British Rail. Fifthly, there are a number of possible quarries outside the Peak
District.

All these matters are of importance in the practicalities of a scheme. Bearing in
mind the limited duration of construction work in any one location - even at the
airport - the installations could be very short-term investments. Clearly if rail
transit was commercially viable, then the chances of it being implemented would be
very great. It is all very well for some environmentalists to advocate such a
course of action for a publicised construction activity, but bearing in mind that
to complete the necessary works at the appropriate receiving end would take time
and therefore delay the start of a contract with a consequential increase in costs,
it requires action by a body not privy to the construction contract, namely,
British Rail. Could the stone quarry supplier, presumably selected as a result of
an open tender, force British Rail to put a siding wherever necessary? Could
British Rail be forced to provide a temporary facility and appropriate plant
erection on their site? The time scale involved in finalising a scheme and inviting
tenders is usually limited when the work suggested by environmentalists and their
political spokesmen requires substantial negotiation and time for implementation.

I set out the above to show that there are these instances where popularist propaganda can whip up support, not to mention the emotions, when the full facts and
the consequential costs are conveniently ignored. The general public do assume at
times that councillors and members of Parliament can deliver the goods, but I
contend that it is downright dishonest to use emotions in this way when it will be
extremely costly to deliver without making the public aware of the full costs of
so doing. Once the costs have been spelled out there is a greater chance that

rational thought rather than sentiment will prevail. Councillors should,
therefore, be careful with their propaganda and be as honest with the public as
they would wish to be with themselves.

The Councillor and Performance Review

In recent years there have been suggestions that Performance Review Committees
should be established as part of the on-going assessment of the council's operation.
This was advocated in the Bains Report, but not all authorities have adopted such
committees, and not all review performance in a meaningful manner.

During the first four years of the Greater Manchester Council, the suggestion for
a Performance Review body was rejected by the majority party. This was possibly
because either the suggestion came from a minority party and therefore acquiescence
would be viewed as capitulation, or because the majority party did not really understand the nature of such a committee and its functions. Needless to say, the submission setting out the proposals stated very clearly what the purpose was to be,
which strengthened my surmise that the first reason was more likely to be near the
truth.

Not all officers viewed the suggestion of such a review with equanimity. They see
a review as a potential threat if ever it should come their way. Yet it is
ironical that since attempts are being made to introduce Management by Objectives
into the public sector which requires a procedure for assessing an individual's
performance against agreed targets, there would seem to be objections to reviewing
the functioning of a department as a whole. The only difference between
councillors undertaking such an appraisal as opposed to an internal management
audit, is the publicity arising from the submission of a report, particularly if it
is adverse or at least not complimentary. Yet local government is open to public
scrutiny and it is inevitable that from time to time criticisms of performance,
justified or not, should be voiced. However, councillors should be aware of the
sensitive nature of such reviews, and avoid the temptation to review an individual's
rather than a department's performance, since the former is a task which should be
undertaken regularly as part of the management function.

It is important that the objectives of such a review body should be clearly spelled
out to provide an appropriate yardstick. The following objectives were set out in
my party's submission to the G.M.C.'s Policy Committee:

1.   To establish that clear political objectives have been laid down; and
(i)   that priorities have been established and followed through; also
(ii)   that the appropriate departments have the requisite structure and resources
       available for fulfilling these objectives.

2.   To review the performance of any project approved by the Council, by
(i)   ensuring that the objectives have been clearly established.
(ii)   that the necessary departmental and interdepartmental structure has
       been clearly defined and is operating effectively.

3.   To review the operation of the department or project on fulfilment of
       the above objectives, with particular reference to procedure, resources
       and financial management.

There are cases - Stockport is one - where investigations are conducted by an
individual member of the Performance Review sub-committee, with the assistance of
the Chief Executive's department. It must be remembered that such reviews, being
inquisitional, are very time-consuming. It is, therefore, essential that members
have sufficient time to devote to this work. There must also be some doubts as to

the wisdom of using a one man inquiry team to conduct such reviews. There are
certainly a number of areas where the involvement of more than one person would be
advisable.

The choice of subject for investigation should be done with care. In some cases,
a Performance Review Committee is used by members to investigate areas of personal
concern which could, as I have experienced, be more in the realms of a feasibility
study rather than that of performance. Feasibility studies should be the responsibility of the officers and not the councillors. Councillors should, therefore, be
wary of instigating anything other than a review of performance. Ideally the
Policy and Resources Committee, under the guidance of the Leader of the Council,
should play a large part in the formulation of these review topics.

There is a need to sound a warning about the manner in which Performance Reviews
are conducted. Each councillor has a special knowledge acquired at his place of
employment and there is a wide spectrum of these skills within a council. If it
is a review of performance rather than a feasibility study which is being undertaken, then it must be undertaken by a councillor with knowledge of that area, or
with substantial research experience. Leslie Chapman in his book "Your Disobedient
Servant" stressed the need to have technologists on his survey teams which were
given the task of effecting economies within his department. He states that
administrators on their own would be quite out of their depth in determining the
potential savings, and he quotes examples where this did not meet with success.

One of the unfortunate traits of accountants and of local government treasurers is
their assumption that knowledge of accounts and accounting methods will uncover
substantial waste. This is not so, as everyone in the construction industry would
testify. If the treasurers had this skill they would have unravelled by now the
problems of over-expenditure on contracts and the increased cost of council houses
over private enterprise (measured on an area basis). The truth of this matter lies
in the manner in which the contracts are awarded and administered, something which
no accounts will reveal. Not only that, accountants are extremely unsuitable for
measuring value for money when it comes to a technical process. This is not to
dismiss the accountancy profession as unsuitable for measuring aspects of performance, but their suitability is strictly limited. This is why Chapman stresses the
need for appropriate technologists to be part of the Performance Review team. I
would support him from my own experience.

It is however possible, if councils will accept the practice of a councillor
having the support of those outside local government but who are conversant with
the process under review.

I have often found a number of people in private enterprise who are engaged in
similar activities such as construction, design, refuse disposal, etc., are able
to supply invaluable data to compare performance of such activities with those of
local government. This is one means whereby lack of expertise with the council
membership can be overcome, although it is preferable to have the expertise within
their ranks, provided those concerned have the discerning mind to undertake such
an investigation, which is not always the case.

Leslie Chapman describes in his book the manner in which Ministers at meetings with
their civil servants made decisions and instructed that directives should be issued
accordingly. Yet, when those directives were issued, they omitted many points made
by the Ministers, some of which were crucial for their implementation. Bearing in
mind that this book is a record, not only of Chapman's achievement, but also of
filibustering by civil servants who are amongst the highest paid civil servants
and are considered by many to be the epitome of perfection throughout the world!
- how much more likely is this situation likely to be repeated within the local

government service? To my knowledge it does occur. Councillors must always be
persistent in seeing the requisite documents which give effect to their decisions,
and above all must devote time to asking penetrating questions to elicit the truth,
rather than accept the official answer which may cover up what officers have either
ignored or not been able to perceive.

Councillors are more fortunate than their parliamentary counterparts in their
ability to meet and discuss matters with the officers concerned. Unfortunately
councillors, being part-time, have less time at their disposal to use this facility.
Nevertheless, it is important that councillors should use every facility available
to them to glean the full facts.

CHAPTER 6

The Effectiveness of Councillors or "Show Him Round But Don't Let Him See!" — The Relationship Between Councillors and Officers

In Chapter 3 mention was made of the possibility of members sitting on Officers' working parties. In one large authority, and possibly in others, members of the majority party attend meetings of the management board or its equivalent. This is an important step towards ensuring that the interaction of policy decisions and managerial implications is fully appreciated. **Councillors** however should insist that this joint working arrangement takes place over a wider field of council activity. The public would be flabbergasted if they were suddenly found with a fifty page document setting out a proposed structure plan for a county. Yet this is precisely the situation which many councillors face. Such a large report, which has been the result of very considerable study by the officers are contin- ually being put before committees, usually with the minimum of notice prior to their consideration by the member. Unless councillors have sufficient free time available before a meeting they are at a loss to comprehend the full extent of such a report. If however a small group of councillors from the appropriate committee sat on the working parties during the gestation period, they would have assimilated all the necessary background thinking and be able to discuss the matter with adequate background knowledge rather than the present system which is based upon either supposition or partial ignorance. It would be appropriate for such a group of councillors to be drawn from all the political parties. Since the final decision will be made by the full committee there is no need for the elected membership of the working party to be in proportion to party representation, because the majority will still be able to exercise control at the full committee meeting.

Some observers may consider such an arrangement to be superfluous. It is a fact of life that when councillors of all shades of opinion are able to take part in prep- aration of reports or have private discussions with the officers or other councillors, a rational rather than a dogmatic approach is possible. I have found from experience that when such approaches are made on a private basis without the glare of publicity, changes do take place.

In addition, it should be remembered that there are many working parties which need not be in continuous session, but receive reports of research etc. from time to time in much the same way that many central government's working parties' advisory committees operate. All that will be required is a transfer of the best practices of central government to the field of local government affairs.

Some officers may assume that they are doing this by issuing periodical reports to the appropriate committees. This can best be described as a token gesture towards member participation. Firstly, the time for study prior to the meeting can be restricted for the reasons previously given, and secondly, such a report invariably forms part of a large agenda with inadequate time being available for a full discussion of the various aspects even of an interim report. In the case of the G.M.C. Structure Plan, there were special seminars held in order to discuss aspects in greater detail than was possible at a committee meeting. The G.M.C. practice is clear evidence of the inadequacy of the regular committee meeting to permit a valid discussion to take place.

There will be the argument that this will make greater calls upon councillors' time particularly during the day when they are usually engaged in earning a living. This is true, but it is a matter which has to be tackled sooner or later if the councillors are to be effective in their task.

A member of the public who attends a council committee or a full council meeting will be horrified at the superficiality of much of the discussion. It is a fact that only about ten per cent of the councillors are really effective in discussion and in contribution at committee or full council meetings. Some never open their mouths. It is not only parliament which has its silent members! This is partly due to the whip system which is discussed later, but also to the sense which some councillors feel of being overwhelmed by paper, and possibly to their inability due to business and other pressures to assimilate the basic documents. A councillo who is silent at meetings can still make a contribution by being the ombudsman for his constituents, or by being a postman between residents and the council. These latter tasks are vital and must not be undervalued. But if they are the only function which a councillor performs - this is true of many of them - then they are failing to fulfil a very major role. Unless joint working groups of councillors and officers are established, the policy decisions will tend to be made by the management team in the manner which was discussed in Chapter 3. More particularly, the roles of councillor and officer will never be understood as that of policy maker and manager respectively. The fact that the roles are often ill-defined in the real life situation is not altogether surprising, since the roles of director and manager in private industry are themselves often blurred, especially when persons hold both posts! An awareness of the separate roles should act as a spur to a re-definition of the roles within an authority and so enable local government to be more effective.

One of the duties of a councillor is to understand the work of the Council over the whole county, borough or district, of which he or she is a member. It is important that there should be visits to activities within the authority to observe its operation at first hand, but also to similar activities elsewhere to help the elected member to be more fully conversant with the environmental problems, conditions, progress of works, etc. This is especially important when some representatives are elected on a very local ticket, typical of ratepayers associations. Once elected, councillors have a duty towards the entire authority and not just their own parish.

Visits can provide a very useful contact which can assist morale amongst employees. It is often a criticism of large enterprises that the men at the top are seldom seen on the shop floor. So it is with many councillors. Their visits do not necessarily have to be formal ones. Many Chief Officers welcome an opportunity to show members what is going on. I have always found extreme friendliness and it is not long before a 'feel' for the morale and the effectiveness of the organisation is obtained.

A sad reflection on the attitude of many councillors is their inability or unwillingness to know not only the staff but the processes involved   I have a vivid

memory of a visit by a council committee to an incineration plant. It was dirty
and smelly. It wasn't long before all but myself had returned to the coach, either
because they found the work there offensive or because lunchtime approached. Yet
if the councillors had remained they would have seen not only some of the mechanic-
problems but the very serious shortcomings of the working sequence and various
other matters which would have enabled them to discuss later in committee in a
knowledgeable manner. Unfortunately too many councillors are just content to use
these visits as a 'works outing'. In consequence, they read report after report,
unable to comprehend the real nature of the operation or the issues which the
reports reveal. Others may find that pressing duties outside local government
give them insufficient time to do such basic research. It is one of the biggest
dilemmas facing local government.

One of the effects of getting to know a number of employees was the opportunity it
gave me to uncover some very undesirable practices. I discovered that an authority
was paying overtime which was not being worked. This followed reports to the
Personnel Committee of overtime working which indicated that some employees were
more than doubling their basic salaries through week-end and other overtime working.
Although statements were made that it was being brought under control, nothing
transpired of any consequence. However, the further discovery that payments were
being made when no work was being carried out was another case. Surveillance was
kept on the situation and as a result a lengthy report was submitted by me covering these matters. *I think my head is expanding*

There were a number of employees at the middle management level who were pleased
that someone was dealing with this and other malpractices, but it appeared to suit
the more senior eschelons to do little or nothing about it. Eventually, there was
no alternative but to refer the matter to the District Auditor. What happened
from there and the involvement of the particular part of the Government service is
dealt with in Chapter 13.

I consider it a basic duty of a councillor to be on the look-out for irregularities
of this and of a similar nature, but it can only be done if the councillor shows an
interest in what is going on, and is inquisitive by nature, able to ask intelligent
questions and, if need be, to probe effectively. In addition, he must be aware of
the possibility of a lame excuse or a potential cover-up.

The chairman of a committee sets the tone for the conduct of operations. If he is
an officers man, the cover-up will usually be effective unless the councillor is
very persistent. If he is an independent chairman, knowledgeable about his domain
of responsibility, he can be sufficiently detached to remedy malpractices and to
ensure adequate performance. I have known both. Unfortunately the latter is the
exception rather than the rule.

How councillors can be misled

It is of course very easy for councillors to be fooled. It is difficult to discern
whether inadequate reports are inadvertently misleading, or a result of profess-
al inadequacy. I once noticed a report to a committee, of which I was not a
member, concerning tenders for a particular type of mechanical plant. The appropriate committee had deemed it advisable to obtain Caterpillar equipment. The
council then went out to tender to two suppliers. It happened that these two
suppliers (of the identical equipment) had concessions from the manufacturer,
which split the authority's area into two. Yet no member of that committee was
aware that the obtaining of the tender was an illusion if they were asking for
competitiveness. The lowest tender came from the supplier whose concessionary
area was largest. I am not questioning the validity of the choice of the particular plant in question; what I do question is the presentation of a report which

gives the innocent the impression that the receipt of the tender was in effect a
truly competitive tender within the spirit of the council's Standing Orders. If
there had been a valid evaluation of alternative types of plant presented to the
committee, it would have been correct to agree to a particular manufacturer,
provided the best possible discounts were made available to the council. In my
judgement I did not believe that this had been done.

One would expect a councillor with an elementary knowledge of the industry concerned to pick up matters of this nature, but few councillors are in such a position.
However, the officers should be. If they are not, it shows a lamentable lack of
commercial knowledge; or if they are, they do local government a disservice by
presenting a report capable of giving a different impression. It is one of the
areas where an individual councillor's knowledge should be used to the full.

Councillors from minority parties should remember that success in debate is not
the key in determining whether the councillor has succeeded in his duties or not!
I have been defeated in resolutions far more often than I have succeeded, but if
the point at issue has been of vital importance to the council's modus operandi, I
have been aware that if the officers accept the validity of the argument they will
change their practices in spite of any outcome in a debate. I believe that I can
truthfully state that on a number of occasions where in practical debate the
resolution has been lost, substantial changes have subsequently been made.

If the public question such practices, they should appreciate that the reason lies
in the relationship between an officer and an elected office holder. The chairman
will, in public debate, defend the current practice to the end, firstly out of a
sense of loyalty to the existing practice, and secondly, out of his own sense of
identity with the department involved. The chairman will of course use the party
whip system to gain support for his view, because a contrary vote will be taken as
a vote of no confidence in him. There are variations to this, such as the device
of a 'reference back', which will be used to enable a different solution to be
presented as one coming from the establishment, rather than from an 'upstart
councillor'. Would-be councillors and those who in opposition feel frustrated
should take comfort from my experience that you 'do not have to win to succeed'.

Councillors sometimes have to be very alert as to the quality of the information
supplied to them. This is particularly true of statistical information, which can
give rise to deductions which fail to reveal the full facts. I witnessed a case
where an abstract of official published statistics was placed before the Refuse
Disposal Sub-committee. The table was entitled "Summary of Refuse Disposal
Statistics 1976/7". The report, in the name of the Chief Officer, discussed the
deployment of manpower and investment. The table was submitted "to give the sub-
committee some indication of the position within the G.M.C. in relation to other
waste disposal authorities. No action is sought nor are any recommendations made
at this time'. It was during the discussion of these statistics that reference
was made by the officers to the favourable position of the G.M.C. in respect of
income per ton. It was so self-congratulating that I was extremely suspicious.
So I later requested to see the original statistics prepared by the Society of
County Treasurers from which they were derived. I set out below the figures as
supplied by the G.M.C. officers, and in the second column the income obtained by
the authority from the sale of reclaimed waste which was not included in the
report.

	Total Income per ton £	Income per ton of reclaimed waste £
Greater Manchester Council	0.32	0.01
West Midland	0.27	0.13
Tyne & Wear	0.42	0.16
West Yorkshire	0.20	0.07
South Yorkshire	0.26	0.06
Merseyside	0.17	0.03
Average for all other Metropolitan Counties	0.20	0.02
Average for all non-Metropolitan Counties	0.20	0.02

While the G.M.C. was second in the league table in respect of the total income per ton (£0.32), it had the lowest figure for income obtained from reclaimed waste. The large income per ton in the case of the G.M.C. was accounted for by the charges made to commercial and industrial undertakings for depositing their refuse at the Council's tips. No officer, bearing in mind these figures were prepared jointly by the Treasurer's and the County Engineer's departments, thought it appropriate to draw any member's attention to this problem area of reclamation. Mind you, if they did they would have had to do some hard appraisal about the problem! Whether the figures prepared by their staff enabled the chief officers concerned to capitalise on them by giving this verbal eulogy of their performance, I cannot be sure.

Some time later, in October 1978, a further set of statistics on Refuse Disposal was presented to the appropriate committee as an appendix to the report. This time there was no reference in the report to the appendix! Once again the correct inference from the study of the original table from which the data in the appendix were extracted (Waste Disposal Statistics based on estimates 1978/9, published by the Society of County Treasurers) was not drawn to the attention of the members by the officers in the report. It showed that the net revenue per ton remained the lowest of the metropolitan counties, and well below the average for the non-metropolitan counties, and that its income was once again derived from the charges for disposal, not from either reclamation or even heat/electricity generation! How long officers will continue to hide the facts from councillors unless the latter have their own private intelligence service will remain a matter of conjecture until there is a re-awakening of their responsibility to use statistical intelligence for the benefit of the community, or perhaps, until they are shamed into action.

What is most distressing about this whole matter is that having raised the issue in 1976 when I served on the Greater Manchester Council, there is a virtual repeat performance two years later. It does call competence on these matters to one's attention, but above all it is clear that it requires far greater in-depth invest-igation by councillors, besides indicating the danger of supplying councillors with summaries of official statistics without expert analysis. Councillors must beware of blind acceptance of data put before them. It is a sad reflection on the operat-ion of local government, but I have been caught out by accepting things at their face value too often not to be chary of such reports.

Early in the life of the Metropolitan Borough of Stockport an exercise was under-

taken by the Corporate Planning Unit. It consisted of an analysis of statistical
data covering all the services of the Authority. There were three such digests,
one for each of the three geographical areas into which the Council is divided.
While the digests were prepared "to provide basic information about specific areas"
they were subsequently used as a means of eliciting from councillors, Community
Councils and the public, suggestions as to the priorities for action.

When the digests were laid before the Area Committee, it was noticeable that most
councillors congratulated the officers on its production and commented on the interesting facts which they contained. They were aghast when the difference between
"interesting" and "useful" facts was pointed out, the latter being the only ones
upon which decisions can be made. None of the statistics produced in these digests
fulfilled this category, yet councillor after councillor was numbed into believing
that he had a basic design-making document before him. The following is an
illustration of the figures contained in the report:-

Extract from Area Digest

Table 17 - County Secondary Schools (Map 8)

Sub Area	No. on map	School	Age Range	Estimated No. of places 1.9.74.
Cheadle	1	Broadway, Cheadle	11-16 Boys	831
	2	Cheadle Grammar, Cheadle Road	11-18 Girls	911
	3	Kingway, Foxland Road	11-16 Girls	756
	4	Moseley Grammar, North Down Road	11-18 Boys	971
				3,469
Bramhall	5	Hazel Grove High Jacksons Lane	11-16 Mixed	1.314
	6	Bramhall High, Seal Road	11-18 Mixed	1,693
	7	Cheadle Hulme High Woods Lane	11-18 Mixed	1,120
				4,127
West Area Total		7 Schools		7,596

There was no information on the number of forms per year, the number of staff, and
many other important items needed to compare the true state of affairs against
known or adjudged targets. Similar insufficient data pervaded the digest, including totals of "Homes for the elderly (Local Authority)". "Homes for the elderly

(Private)", but without any yardstick to assess the possible shortfall in provision of such accommodation both now or in the future. The population statistics only related to the 1971 census. There was no projections for later years. How could councillors or others make any judgement, therefore, as to the priority for such accommodation as against new schools, additional teachers, etc.? No, it was a simple case of the authority being unable to identify the statistical information upon which to base any meaningful decision. In certain cases it would have been appropriate to use national norms of elderly persons' accommodation per 1000 of population over 65, together with estimated projection of the retired population to identify the true nature of the problem areas requiring decisions and, in particular, the priorities for expenditure.

Whether the reaction of the councillors to this and similar documents is yet another testimonial to the lack of basic managerial type expertise is a matter for the reader to judge. Bearing in mind the salaries paid to the compilers of the tables, the reader may also obtain an impression of the quality of the expertise available!

Little wonder, however, that the impression gains ground that the best way to be-muse or pre-occupy elected representatives is to blind them with figures! I shall be putting forward in Chapter 9 a different approach which calls for the present-ation of statistics in such a way that the people rather than things become the basis from which data are collected and decisions taken.

The abuse of the Party Whip

The larger councils have eliminated the tri-partisan approach to local government found in the former smaller authorities. It could be argued that the limited number of councillors in the smaller authorities precluded one party from filling all the posts from within its own ranks without overburdening their own members with excessive responsibilities. It did, however, help to establish in a number of instances a real forum for debate on issues rather than on party dogma. I remember engaging in heated debate against the views of a committee chairman from my own party when we were in the minority on the council! I know it shocked some political animals while no doubt delighting members of other parties bent on party one-upmanship!

Whatever system is adopted, there is always the possibility of abuse. Democracy is open to abuse as much as any other form of government. All forms of government must provide for decision-taking. Management which only operates through a system of "management by committee" has a grave danger of drifting into ineptitude. Therefore the party whip system is seen by many to be essential to the decision-making process. The gravest danger to democracy lies in the use of the party whip system as a tool of a ruling clique, preventing the expression of dissent or even disquiet amongst those subservient to that whip.

There is a fundamental difference between the whip system used by the two major parties and that used by the Liberals. It is believed in certain political circles that a Conservative party candidate has to commit allegiance to the Sovereign, the Party and the whip in that order. There is no doubt that the effect of the whip on Conservative members is very severe on those who are of an independent mind. This is not to say that those who have stood as paper candidates and have subsequently been elected do not find the receipt of instructions as to attitudes to adopt and to the way in which to vote very convenient; but the silencing of elected members by the whip system remains a threat to democracy. It is easy for those of us in the Liberal Party to observe such events. In the case of Stockport, the Borough has a system, to be discussed later, of area committees where all the elected members of a defined area meet to discuss matters of concern to that area. It has not been infrequent to witness Conservative members voting one way at the area committee meeting (which has no executive powers) and, at the later service committee of the council to find them silenced and voting in a contrary fashion without explanation as to their change of heart! It should be appreciated that the area committees are open to the public and are often well-attended because local people find it easier to travel to these meetings than to the Town Hall. If the subject concerns a planning application it subsequently goes to a sub-committee which is not open to the public, but which makes the effective decision. Any change of mind from that given at the area committee therefore remains hidden within the exclusive club of the sub-committee unless there is a recorded vote. Such changes of mind are the direct result of the imposition of the party whip. There is a strong case for arguing that where such a situation arises through the whip system, that it is a negation of democracy which can ultimately destroy any sense of confidence between the elector and the elected member.

My impression from a study of the Conservative group behavious on councils is that there is within each group a powerful clique in the form of its own policy committee which is the determining body of that party's policy, and wherever they have control, they direct and control the whole council programme through the party whip system. In 1976 during the financial crisis which hit local government, a decree was issued by the then leader of the council that there should be a 10% cut across the board of all expenditure. Although strong advice, I gather, was given to the party caucus of the dangers of such a blanket instruction upon certain operations and, in particular on the maintenance of council property, that decision was forced through the internal party machine and then subsequently by the use of its majority through the Council without any comment by the protesters within their own party. Party unity has become a sacred cow.

There was another instance where was the central directive from the Tory Shadow Secretary of State to close down as an economy measure the Advice Centres which form part of the Consumer Protection Service. Ironically the policy of establishing such centres was laid down by a colleague when he was the Secretary of State! There was pressure to ignore this direction exerted on the council leader by members of his own party who, when in opposition, had supported the establishment of these centres. Incidentally, the savings to the ratepayers would have been nil, as these centres received a 100% grant from central Government. Yet the Conservatives delayed action on one centre in Stockport which was never opened, as explained in Chapter 8, although the County Council had taken a long lease for which the ratepayers are paying £10,000 a year, and due to the centre being non-operational it did not attract grant aid! It could be claimed that this was an instance where the inner party caucus failed to succeed in closing the centres and therefore showed that democracy can sometimes come alive, yet it took some twelve months to resolve the issue during which the staff involved suffered a lowering of morale due to this uncertainty within the majority party. It is illustrative of the inner workings of the Conservative group and shows clearly that democracy, where it does exist, is only kept alive in the private party meetings behind closed doors, and that the full committee meeting held in the glaze of publicity is little more than a charade.

The saga involving the establishment of a major modern theatre in Manchester is really a story of a power struggle within the Conservative group. As with other major projects planned by the G.M.C. when under Labour control, the Conservative position was either one of support or of complete silence. I never heard of any fundamental opposition by the Conservatives to the major reconstruction of the Manchester Opera House, yet when they assumed control, the Conservatives ditched the scheme and subsequently, due to the intervention of others such as the Arts Council, decided on the Palace Theatre.

Equally the volte-face on the Piccadilly to Victoria underground scheme is another
example of political dogma laid down by the party caucus of the present Conservative majority. This scheme, designed to provide a through rail link between the
city's southern and northern networks with an inner distribution system, was supported by all parties and presented as an all-party project to successive Conservative and Labour Ministers. Yet when the Tory party caucus secured control of
the council it overturned all the plans and all support previously expressed by
their rank and file was silenced through the operation of the party whip. The
Labour party has a not dissimilar modus operandi within it, but there is a strong
impression that it lacks much of the dictatorial nature of the Conservative caucus,
a leading member of which has stated his belief in dictatorship rather than effective democracy! I have witnessed occasions when the Labour group has withdrawn the
obligation to submit to the party whip. This is not frequent, but its occurence
gives hope that the individual's commitments to his own opinion counts for more
than is the case in the Conservative party. This is not to say that attacks from
outsiders on their policy does not bring out a deep sense of loyalty which will
override individual feeling, but the willingness to air certain differences in
public rather than confine differences to meetings held behind closed doors, gives
hope to those who wish to see a greater freedom of expression and honest discussion
within the Council Chamber.

The Liberal Party, in my experience, does not operate behind closed doors. On the
other hand, on the Greater Manchester Council, there was an invitation (only one
paper took it up) for the press to be present, and we never imposed any restrictions
on publication of these group meetings. We often respected different opinions
amongst our members who then decided whether to abstain, or to vote contrary to
the majority. Cynics might claim that since we were not in power, we could afford
this procedure as a luxury. They are entitled to their view, but I surmise that
if the alternative was put to the electorate as to the method whereby they should
be governed, they would prefer the Liberal approach.

Any system can be abused if its operators so desire, but the effect of the party
whip system in local government is to place power in the hands of a small clique
and above all to give a false front to the public. The latter is probably the
reason why so many leaks to the press occur. Premature disclosures of certain
plans has politically scuppered some schemes being prepared for bulldozing through
both the committees and the council in cases where they are based either on
political dogma or on inadequate facts. The secrecy surrounding the operation of
the party caucus and its associated whip system runs counter to the desire of many
people for a more open style of government.

One of the most disturbing features of the use of the party whip system is the
silencing of voices within a group. I have experienced occasions when, as
Liberals, we have put forward proposals for change, documented them, (the proposal
for a Performance Review Committee as outlined in Chapter 5 was one of many such
examples) to discover from private conversation with members of other parties
support, only to find that the ruling caucus has viewed such proposals as a threat
to their position of power and consequently issued a three line whip to oppose
such schemes.

The only other alternative to ensure implementation is to use private discussions
without publicity except for the occasions when it comes before the council as part
of the programme of the majority party. Such is the nature of politics that it
becomes essential never to give credit or credence to the views and suggestions of
others! This feature of political life whether local or national does deter a
number of people from being involved in the active political arena, thereby reducing the calibre of a councillor.

The Council's patronage

There is a widespread notion that once elected you are entitled to serve on a number
of bodies as a representative of the electorate, thereby in some people's eyes
spreading democratic control of otherwise self-perpetuating or independent bodies.
They range from the Courts of Universities through to such organisations as Tourist
Boards, various charities, Sports Councils, to local government organisations such
as the Association of Metropolitan Authorities (or appropriate body) and its
associated committees. It is possible to regard School Managers as being included
in this list, but they do tend to have one difference. School Managerships are
usually distributed throughout all parties represented on the council, and to those
schools of the particular area which the councillor represents. In other cases,
there are a certain number of bodies where the designation of the appointees are
automatic, like the Chairman of a Committee, and possibly the appropriate Director
on a related body such as the Advisory Councils for Further Education. In Stockport
there are one hundred such appointments, together with nearly one hundred and fifty
school managerships on offer. The school managerships which can be regarded as
being an integral post of the authority's educational system. Although the continuous determination to swamp such bodies with a surplus of councillors even if they
are from other areas, seems to run counter to the concept of local involvement in
the various schools. They do have one advantage in that the minutes of the
Managers' meeting do find their way into local government machinery by being
reported to the Educational committee. No such arrangements exist for the other
numerous external bodies on which councillors serve. Maybe the business of the
appropriate committee could be weighed down by their inclusion. What is clear is
the total absence in the case of their outside bodies of any accountability of the
councillor's stewardship.

Some of the outside bodies do not help in this matter. Some universities, for
example, have the Mayor and the Chairman of the Education Committee of an authority
as ex-officio members. Since Mayors are invariably annual appointments, the opportunity for continuity and the making of an effective contribution is seriously
reduced. It could be contended that such bodies as the Universities have deluded
those to whom they submit their charters for approval into believing that they are
effectively involving the community in their work! For the Universities at least
it provides an effective cover behind which they can proceed on their way, unhamp-
ered by external interference. Another feature of this quango type appointment is
that it is in the great majority of cases confined to the membership of the majority party, as if this was the privilege available to those in power, in the same
way as Ministers are able to exercise their patronage in appointments entrusted to
them. What is more disastrous probably for the bodies concerned, there is no guar-
antee that the appointee is even remotely interested in the activity concerned, or
even has the time to be fully involved in the activities concerned. There are
some organisations which strike it lucky, but in the majority of cases it is a
matter of accepting what comes up with the rations!

There are a limited number of organisations who are keen to have local councillors
as their members. Councils for voluntary services are a case in point. Such
organisations consider that councillors can then become successful advocates on
their behalf for grants from the appropriate authority. Whether such an arrangement has any success depends upon the calibre of councillors. In some cases, to
add weight to the body's voice, the Councillor is made Chairman of that body, so
that he becomes the embodiment of the organisation and is duty bound to defend it
to his or her last breath!

Many appointments are sinecures and there is a need to prune the list considerably.
There will be a suggestion that these appointments do little or no harm and in the

current mood of apathy should therefore be accepted. However, whether councillors
so appointed make any valuable contribution to the working of such an organisation
depends upon the luck of the draw and which party has councillors of ability to
perform effectively. Others, such as the Consumer's Consultative Councils, are a
valuable means of bringing public pressure to bear upon nationalised industries.
Here again there have been examples of political patronage ousting persons of
ability from its membership, due to unacceptable (to the majority party) political
affiliations, but in one or two cases to the credit of these councils they have
sought to co-opt such victims of modern nepotism.

The need for reform is clear and it should take the form of severe pruning of the
lists. The system should be used to match personal interests and abilities, regardless of party, with the appropriate posts together with a more effective means of
making such appointees accountable for their stewardship.

There are many councillors, and members of Parliament for that matter, who are
successful in retaining their seats by looking after the immediate needs of their
constituents, taking up the broken pavements and inadequate workmanship, etc., but
who nevertheless never achieve any radical change for their constituents. Some
members of Parliament have represented derelict areas and even after twenty years
the position is little changed. It creates the impression that some have a vested
interest in dereliction otherwise their seats could be in jeopardy! A similar
situation exists for some councillors.

Such councillors are successful in dealing with the minutae, and to this end are
ably supported by numerous officers who find it easier to deal with yesterday's
problems rather than next year's priorities. Both councillor and officer are able
to play the same game but for different reasons. The councillor is seen as an
effective 'local refuse collector', while the officer is able by satisfying the
needs of his political masters to devote his time to pursuing his own policies and
programmes with the minimal interference.

The creation of the new metropolitan counties effected a major change for a number
of elected members. The new counties are basically strategic planning organisations far removed from the tactical tasks of the districts. As such the counties
require officers and members who are capable of comprehending long-term plans and
considerations, which is a skill given to too few. Councillors who are unable to
fulfil this role complain that the county authorities are too remote, and thereby
expose their own weakness to fulfil this role. It is not that the counties are
too remote, but that their tasks concern the total environment as they conceive it
ten to twenty years hence, when many of the councillors will either be put out to
grass or will have passed on. It is the inability of many councillors, coupled
with a number of officers, to look this far ahead that thwarts long-term schemes
such as the National Ice Skating Centre, and Manchester's need for a rail link
between the northern and southern parts of the city. The number of schemes such
as those dating back to the rapid transit system for Wythenshawe in the south, to
Langley in the north, that have been scrapped on the altar of immediate public
econ.omy is an eloquent testimonial to the inability of the modern democratic
process to throw up men of stature with vision. This is not to decry the democratic process, but to point out to the electors that the true effectiveness of both
members of Parliament and councillors is what they leave behind in ten years' time
and not to-day's state of play.

The effectiveness of a councillor therefore can only be judged by the criteria of
his ability to do some forward thinking and planning along with the officers.
Accordingly he requires to be serviced by persons with this ability. It is not a
common gift and therefore the ranks of the public servants will have to be scoured
to find suitable staff to back up this function. At present such a councillor is

hampered by firstly the inadequate training of staff capable of undertaking long-term planning, and secondly, by the desire of many staff within local authorities to see their priorities for action being to maintain existing levels of employment amongst themselves, rather than the former concept of public service which was certainly the hallmark of many an urban or rural district of yesteryear.

The truly effective councillor needs to equip himself with modern managerial skills so that he can detect the present weaknesses within the paid service of the council, and to inject a managerial approach into the total organisation of the authority. Such a situation has not come about through the re-organisation of 1974, nor will it unless both the will and the ability exists amongst the elected members. The effectiveness of a councillor therefore depends upon his ability to equip himself to be the master of events and the initiator of policies, rather than the rubber stamp of a self-perpetuating bureaucracy to which the status quo provides a comfortable bed with a supporting mattress of high pay and not inconsiderable fringe benefits.

CHAPTER 7

Financial Accountability — "We Have Slipped Again"

It is not the intention to discuss in this chapter the details of the various sources of local government, or to suggest alternative solutions to those put forward by the Layfield Committee which went into this detail, although some limited comment is made. The intention is to discuss the effectiveness or otherwise of financial accountability within an authority, this in turn reflects on the ability of a councillor to monitor performance in financial terms.

There are a limited number of services provided by a local authority which arise out of house-occupancy as such and which incur costs regardless of the number of inhabitants. They include such items as refuse collection and the use of the highway adjoining the property. The vast majority of services, however, incur costs which are proportional to the number of inhabitants. These include education, which takes the lion's share of a local authority's budget, certain social services and aspects of environmental health. Although responsibility for water supplies has been taken out of the hands of local authorities, it is another item which is based upon rateable value, and assumes greater importance as the various charges escalate. The Water Rate has risen faster than the indices produced by economists to assess the cost of living. The burden of the ever-increasing water rates levied bears particularly hard upon certain sections of the community such as the elderly and single parent families, who have fixed incomes or little earning potential. It is inevitable that as the rise in the general rate continues that there will be an increasing use of the rate rebate scheme. With the increasing numbers of elderly people, this will not only make the pressure for rebates greater, but calls for the water rate to be included in the rate rebate schemes. The present position becomes even more farcical due to the separate arrangement for levying the Water Rate, now outside democratic control, but also because water consumption is a function of the number of occupants rather than the size of the building.

The reliance upon the present system of rates as the sole means, save for direct government grants, for financing local expenditure, has gone beyond the bounds of all reason and applied common sense. It is also pertinent to comment that every time ad hoc devices such as rate rebates are introduced to alleviate hardship, another addition is made to the burden ratepayers face due to the additional administration it necessitates, which in turn means that once again it falls heaviest upon the least able to bear it. We are in fact slowly gathering speed as we turn in ever-decreasing circles to be sucked down into a bureaucratic bedlam.

The failure of the Layfield Committee to recommend alternative methods of raising money for local government is a major setback for all who believe that the present system is inadequate in present society. The absence of any form of revenue to a local authority which is, as economists express it, income elastic, is the root cause of much of the anguish felt by the majority of ratepayers, and which in turn makes local government a needless target for complaints and derision. While the central government benefits from the increased taxation obtained from increased earnings, many people on fixed incomes have to pay an ever-increasing proportion for a service which in time can only deteriorate as far as they are concerned. The elderly feel that it is particularly hard, as having educated their children, they have to bear the increasing costs of educating others!

We now possess sophisticated equipment such as computors to solve complex problems, yet we seem completely unable to find any satisfactory solution to the system of raising revenue for local government! Such is the state of our development as a nation!

The problems which councils face in determining financial programmes is compounded by the fact that a substantial proportion (approximately 50%) comes from central government, which each year can decide to switch financial support from one type of authority such as the metropolitan areas to others such as the shire counties at a political whim, or, as the cynics would suggest, according to the electoral prospects. Further, the decision as to the size of central government grants etc. is made very late in the preparation stage of the council's budget for the forth-coming year.

A substantial part of the capital expenditure is financed by long-term loans. 91% of the capital expenditure in 1978-9 in Greater Manchester was financed by these loans. We therefore get the endless circle of central government raising taxes to provide money for local authorities to pay back by way of loans!

The inability to make long-term financial prediction, on a sound basis, does hamper forward planning. This becomes more acute as inflation continues at an unacceptable level! Little wonder that November to March each year is the silly season for financial prediction by local authorities. Figures of potential percentage increases in the rates are branded about as if there is a public game of table tennis going on with the central government and opposition parties all joining in at one stage or another to batter the ratepayer as if he is the table tennis ball.

Setting aside, therefore, the difficulties of determining the amount that the national government provides the authority through the Rate Support Grant, it is appropriate to make some comments on the budgetting process itself. There is always a base from which future expenditure has to be assessed. This is the commitment in the form of debt charges and the balance of current capital schemes to be completed. Amongst the local authorities of Greater Manchester, it accounts in 1978-9 for 17% of the total revenue expenditure. When interest charges vary with the frequency that has been our experience in recent years, the problem of accurate budgetting is increased. In times of financial stringency, opportunities to engage in major projects such as increased Social Services to cope with an ageing population including the provision of appropriate housing are few, and they are not helped by the burden of debt which can be for a long term, such as 60 years. Seldom, if ever, is there a capital rate levy to finance projects to prevent this ever-increasing burden of debt from strangulating the inauguration of future schemes.

The argument that a mortgage debt incurred to-day becomes proportionately less as the income of those at work increases over time, does not apply to local government unless the amount of money extracted from the long-suffering ratepayers is increased. Under the present system of financing capital programmes through long-term loans, this proportion will increase rather than decrease as more and more capital schemes are started.

One of the features of local authority budgetting is the attitude to the budget itself. In some instances it is a statement of intent to spend with subsequent approval of the various schemes when they are ready for implementation. In others, it becomes a licence to a committee to spend within the budgetted figure.

The latter case is most likely to arise when the budget meeting is concerned with policy options which have financial implications. It is very neat and tidy to do this, but the budget meeting results from some six months' deliberations over schemes which are put into these policy options. It is only some three months before the final approval of the budget when these policy options are formulated, that the authority is likely to know the amount to be received through the Rate Support Grant, which together with the existing rate levy, establishes at least a fixed sum by way of income. But by this time the commitment to spend money on new projects is well advanced and there is a reluctance to back-track, especially when in order to fulfil the proposed programme some preliminary work will in all probability have been carried out.

If the Government decided to advance the date of its fixing of the Rate Support Grant to July or August in respect of the following financial year, it would be possible to establish the priorities for schemes with a known income from existing sources. It would then be possible to know the cost in terms of an increased rate levy of an extra scheme. At the moment it is the schemes which determine the rate levy, rather than the anticipated income determining which scheme, if any, would be included in the council's programme.

It is pertinent to point out at this stage that local authorities are often keen to employ personnel themselves rather than use the services of others, such as contractors on fixed term contracts. For instance, it is perfectly feasible to have a dog warden scheme operated under contract, which can be terminated in accord- ance with the terms of a contract, without the necessity of an on-going commitment in the form of permanent employees operating as dog wardens. This obsession with Do-it-Yourself rather than contracting, is another reason why so much of local government budgetted expenditure is based on a continuing commitment due to the establishment of posts, rather than a re-assessment of the priority of the service being provided. In the case of a dog warden service, if the problem of stray dogs is severely reduced, the priority for that expenditure would drop, and could be diverted to another of a higher priority. In this way, much of the service provided by authorities could be improved and made flexible to meet needs at a given time. The present inflexibility created by direct labour is a curse, but it is often extended by councils under socialist control, although when the conser- vatives take over there seems to be little reduction in the fundamental approach to employing personnel by the councils themselves.

A typical example of this occurred when the design team was set up to prepare for the construction of the second runway at Manchester Airport. At the Personnel Committee I challenged the establishment of a separate unit for this work. I proposed an amendment that once it was designed, it would be possible to deploy the staff - or at least most of them - on other projects, and not to have them as on-going financial commitments regardless of the workload! The curse of fixed establishments is that they are almost unalterable till vacancies arise when it is possible to disestablish posts, but the interval during which one waits for retirement or promotion is unpredictable and can be both expensive in time and expensive in rates.

Local authorities split their expenditure into Capital and Revenue items. This

arises due to the different ways of financing schemes. Capital Schemes are viewed
by the central government as if they have no revenue implications. This is
particularly true in the construction field. It is perfectly possible to spend
additional money on a capital building project which will save revenue costs at a
later date, and which, if carried out, would in a relatively short term pay for
itself. The need to restrict capital costs in school construction, for example,
has resulted in considerable expenditure in repair work out of all proportion to
the original cost within some ten to fifteen years of the initial building.

However much local authorities might wish to ensure effective financial control by
examining the combined capital and revenue costs together, they are stymied by the
central government defining the allocation of items into the two categories to
suit its own administrative convenience, rather than any desire to establish the
true total costs of capital projects. This division is even more disastrous for
local government, since it treats design work as a revenue cost unless the capital
scheme has been approved. The absence of any clear identity of design costs is
clear to see in the new scheme designed to provide the type of forward transportation planning known as the Transport Policies and Programme (T.P.P.). It is a
five year rolling programme, of which this is a typical extract:-

"Estimated Expenditure (Nov. 1975 prices)
(£'000s)

		1976-7	1977-8	1978-9	1979-80
Southern Internal	Works	400	1800	2000	136
By-pass Oldham	Land	300	-	-	- "

Yet in spite of the T.P.P. system, governments themselves plan their own motorway
programme of financial expenditure on an annual basis, and they are prone to switch
expenditure authorisation from one scheme to another late in the financial year if
one or other scheme hits a delay. They make the assumption that the scheme simply
requires the awarding of a contract, totally ignoring design work and its costs,
and often assuming that a whole series of designs languish in the bottom drawer of
the designer's office! It is not surprising that Highway Authorities, jealously
seeking the right to spend monies, prepare designs for schemes even outside the
five year time scale of the T.P.P., in the hope that they will be the recipients of
government largesse at the last minute of the financial year! How can a councillor
in such circumstances exercise any effective control over design costs in these
departments? Not until the cost of design is seen as an integral part of capital
projects will there be any financial control over this important phase, which will
remain to be borne by the rates.

I once challenged the County Engineer on the vast number of schemes inherited by
the new county authority upon re-organisation. The answer I received was to the
effect that there were new features and they would have to be done again!
Apparently amendments to the initial schemes were unacceptable because the design
criteria of former authorities were now unacceptable to the new authority. Such is
the one-upmanship of designers! The cost of these unused designs is never reported
to the council, however, nor do many councillors understand the system and what it
costs.

The planning and control of capital projects by local authorities is still in its
infancy as far as development of effective procedures are concerned. Looking again
at the extract of the T.P.P. referred to earlier, it is argued by some officers
that setting out a timescale of this nature makes it too rigid, bearing in mind the
complexities of the process needed to complete the final scheme, and therefore some
inbuilt flexibility is desirable. There is a valid argument for a plan which by
its complex nature requires considerable flexibility built into the programme,

provided there are effective controls. Unfortunately there seldom are. When the
schemes are inserted in the T.P.P. there is no appraisal of the timescale needed
for the processes leading up to the possession of the site by the contractor, so
inevitably time and again the actual occurrence of expenditure in the case cited
moves from 1976-7 to 1979-80 and possibly into 1980-81. Local government has a
special jargon word for this - slippage!

The financial slippage, which occurs due to planned expenditure taking place in a
later year, is a recurrent feature of local government finance. Local government
seems incapable of attaching any accuracy to its financial forecasts of capital
works. This is fundamentally not a failure by the treasurers, but a failure of
corporate management to effectively plan and control a capital programme. There
are very few officers specifically delegated to monitor the capital programme, as
might be expected with the establishment of the post of Chief Executive, who in
his management role should be held responsible for this task. The argument which
I have heard being bandied across the table is that there are insufficient staff,
yet no one from outside the Chief Officer's domain - not even an elected member -
goes in to ensure that staff who are working on minor non-priority work which
could be delayed, are transferred to the priority tasks to give effect to the
committed programme.

Due to the fact that design work is not shown as part of a capital programme, there
is a complete absence of any report on the state of progress on the design work of
the various capital projects. I suspect that money is being spent on design work
which is not yet in the forward plan of the authorities, and that much of it, as
stated earlier, could be abortive.

It would be assumed that budget preparation would be the appropriate time for the
review of the whole of the Council's operation, section by section. Unfortunately
the opportunity for councillors to review aspects of activities and their financial
implications is stilted, not only by the time available for committee meetings, but
also by the paucity of information supplied. Experience shows that budget time is
planned expenditure time, and not for a review of performance. Everything that has
money spent on it, every activity which is current, is automatically assumed to be
on-going, and therefore forms the base data upon which future expenditure on staff
and projects is planned. Local government has a wonderful facility for expanding
its workload to overflow its accommodation! Budget time is never used to assess
any possible retrenchment in activity; that only comes with crises, when moratoriums
on staff recruitment and postponements of the starts of projects arise. Local
authorities just do not have the ability to effect retrenchment; for each on-going
activity is a sacred cow! Even if time is too short when the annual budget is
prepared, councils never take the opportunity to carry out a major review of
performance later in the councils' year.

This is not the only problem facing any effective review. Since central government
looks at revenue and capital as two separate items requiring different methods of
financing, few councils in preparing their expenditure options isolate that proportion of revenue expenditure which arises from debt charges.

If a leisure activity such as a municipal theatre is to be validly appraised, there
is a need to know the total breakdown of revenue expenditure and income, together
with any capital expenditure. Only in this way can the level of subsidy or income
be validly assessed. If it is disguised, as it is on so many occasions, by providing a combined revenue figure which includes the debt charges, it is extremely
difficult to make realistic judgments on the viability of the activity. Worse
still, such a presentation completely diverts the councillor's attention away from
those areas where decisions are clearly desired.

It is of course open to the councillors to demand that the information is presented in a meaningful manner, but the diehard traditionalists on both the members' and the officers' sides make the process of adjustment extremely laborious. It is indicative of the very slow progress by public authority accountants towards the use of modern management techniques and financial data presentation.

The absence of management accounting and the provision of financial data for policy and management decisions is an everyday occurrence in local government. Time and again, requests are made at both committee and full council meetings for data on such items as the cost of waste paper collection, only for members to be told that staff cannot be spared to provide this information! Councils have spent thousands of pounds in the provision of computers which seem mainly used for totting up the wages and preparing accounts for auditors. Seldom, if ever, are programmes developed and used which enables councils to monitor progress, or provide information to test the financial viability of policies.

There is a danger that the use of computers by the authorities has created a built-in inflexibility. In one case wages for school crossing patrols were paid in the middle of the month, up to the end of the month. Yet this service suffered from a very high turnover of staff. A number of staff left in the first week of the month, having been paid till the end of it, which necessitated the authority clawing it back! Would it be impossible to make weekly giro payments? Or might it complicate the system too much?

The production of productivity indices in respect of direct works operation is something almost unheard of. Yet data of this kind is essential if councillors are going to keep an eye on the effectiveness of these departments. In one case I discovered that bonus payments were regarded as overheads! If the accounting procedures require this (and I don't know the reason why), then how can anyone monitor the effect of bonus schemes on unit costs? I get some very strange answers from local authority accountants. If, for example, there is a planned maintenance scheme based upon bonuses, I am told that if the productivity goes up, the cost to the authority will increase because more materials will be used! If there is a fixed sume for repairs, then if productivity increases (and surely this should be encouraged) then there is less need to employ as many staff. But no, it appears that this is not the objective. The reasoning appears to go as follows: we have a fixed sum, if we improve productivity we will be able to do more work. This means that we will exceed the budget. So we don't have planned maintenance schemes in case productivity rises!!

The present state of public accounting indicates that the major emphasis of the treasurer's duties still lies in the simple book-keeping process. There is very little evidence that local authorities have developed similar techniques of managerial accounting to those used in the private sector. If they do, few councillors see the fruits of such labours, otherwise much this is amiss in local government would be effectively planned, monitored, and above all, controlled.

CHAPTER 8

District - County Relations or "Pass the Buck Whenever Possible"

There has always been consultation between the two tiers of government of County and District. There were certain county functions which were delegated to municipal boroughs and to the urban and rural districts, but these varied within certain counties. It could, therefore, be logically held by the supporters of the Local Government Act 1972, that the inception of the Highway Agency Agreements under that Act were an extension and formalisation of a system already in existence. The establishment of a universal two-tier system which eliminated the previous single-tier county boroughs, presented a situation alien to a large number of elected members and to the officers of these former county boroughs. To say that the new lower tier resented the removal of some of these former powers is to express it in mild terms judging by the reactions which still persist. This resentment is acute where the new district councils in the metropolitan areas, such as the City of Manchester, were virtually unchanged in size compared with their former independent status as county boroughs. Other new authorities formed round former county boroughs, but substantially increased in size, reacted less sharply to these diminutions of power, but suspicions still exist.

Re-organisation created a number of concurrent functions in addition to the possibility of a Highways Agency Agreement whereby the district act as agents for the County which remained the Highway Authority. The establishment of the agency agreement is at the discretion of the county. Leaving aside for the time being the concurrent functions of planning, land acquisition and many activities in the field of recreation and arts, the decision to operate a Highways Agency Agreement could have a profound effect upon staffing levels and career structure for those involved in Highway engineering. If there is no agency agreement whereby certain functions, especially design work, could be carried out by the district councils, the concentration of expertise and activity within the county council could result in a top heavy department with possible dissipation of effort. From the staff point of view there would be a curtailment of career opportunities within the county area. It could also stifle internal criticism and initiative. Therefore the decision of the G.M.C. to enter into such agreements with its ten districts provided an opportunity for the district councils to employ design staff on projects up to a certain value. This provided a certain esprit-de-corps amongst the district's engineering staff and enhanced their status. It also has allowed staff to move from one district to another in a freer market than would have been the case without such an agreement.

No arrangement can be without its dangers and it is up to those who operate it to

do so in a spirit of maturity and not in one motivated by jealousy. The worst
features of such an agency agreement are exposed when it becomes the vehicle to
permit officers of both authorities to pass the buck of true accountability from
one to another.

Reference was made in Chapter 2, when discussing staffing, to the problems of
traffic management which arose out of the agency agreement. Decisions on Traffic
Orders come within the preview of the County Engineer, yet these are generated at
local level and are required to solve local problems. The mechanism whereby these
are effected is very cumbersome. In Stockport these are discussed at the Area
Committee meeting, which is the appropriate point at which these matters should be
discussed and probably initiated. The suggested traffic orders are then sent to
the district council's traffic Regulation Sub-committee, where the advice of the
engineering representatives of the County Engineer is available, then to the works
committee, to the full council, and subsequently to the traffic regulations sub-
committee of the county to be endorsed or rejected by its highways committee and
full council! Some seven committees could be involved; whether they are discussed
in detail at each depends upon the extent of representations which are made. At
least it can be claimed that there is an opportunity for a full hearing! Yet this
is in addition to all the statutory procedures and notices that are required before

If there was an effective means of delegation, there would be no need for the
matter to be referred to the county committees. I contend that the County Engineer,
if he supported the recommendation of his own staff who are avilable at district
traffic meetings, could give his authorisation, having satisfied himself that the
district council had completed all the statutory duties, served the necessary
notices and complied with an established procedure. Such a system would avoid the
duplication that exists at county level and so provide an opportunity to reduce
the salary bill, which continues to be inflated in this way.

Passing the buck is almost a national pastime. When it is difficult to determine
who in fact makes the final decision it becomes very frustrating. On one occasion
members of an area committee were convinced that a minor road scheme processed by
the district council and included in its programme of minor works was unnecessary,
and would create additional traffic problems including increased speed. They
conveyed their opinion by resolution to their district council, only to be told by
the officers that the scheme was approved by the county which had the ultimate
sanction, yet those of us who served on the county council also challenged the
necessity of the scheme, only to be told that since the district council had put in
its list of proposals, the county agreed to include it within the districts'
financial allocation for expenditure on road schemes! This buck passing was aided
and abetted by the two different cycles of meetings of the two councils, which
ensured that it was difficult to refer it back. The casual observer may be tempted
to believe that even where there is a concensus between the local county and
district councillors on such schemes, the mechanism of an agency agreement does
permit the officers to'play the ball from end to end', as it were, in order to
achieve their own private objectives. But the whole process does give rise to
questions as to the true location of the point of decision making under the agency
agreement system. Unfortunately when you have chairmen, who become the political
mouthpieces of their technical officers, the difficulty of identifying the true
decision maker is blurred by the political hold of the chairman over their own
majority party members, which often acts as a block to their ability to remain
sufficiently independent of mind to view the situation dispassionately.

There is, in addition, a financial complication which plays its part in the continued confusion which exists under some agency agreements. Sums are allocated to be
spent in a particular financial year. When the viability or the necessity of
schemes are challenged, the answer comes back, "this money has been allocated. We

have no other schemes ready. If we don't spend it, we will lose the money from
the County and they will cut our allocation next year. Therefore to safeguard our
future allocations we must spend now." There is a strong suspicion that this attitude is adopted by some officers to further their own preferred options. The situation is helped by officers attempting to set one council off against another.
It is a not uncommon occurrence. One such situation concerned street lighting
improvements. There are many areas where a policy of 'new lamps for old' takes
place. New taller posts are installed which require greater power than would be
the case if the old, but shorter, existing lamp posts were fitted with a modern
filament to reduce the running costs. This replacement programme of both filaments
and standards takes place often where there are reasonable lighting levels, rather
than in those areas where there are often old inadequate lighting systems for a
less well used road. The county sets aside a sum in its budget for street lighting
improvements for each district. Whether the district or the county officers
decide the exact roads where the work is to take place is also difficult to determine. One council's officers will say that it is the other council's technical
staff.

The Highway Agency scheme has much to commend it, provided there is adequate delegation under the agreement to the districts to make the decisions, and to be fully
accountable to their own councillors. As stated earlier, if the County Engineer,
as the responsible officer, disagrees, he should discuss it with the district's
own committee, and only in case of dispute between himself and the district committee refer it back to his own council. If this was done, not only would many
purely local decisions be made by those who are closest to the problem, but it
would save considerable time, and dare I say it, cut the amount of paper work.

There are clearly certain decisions which need to be made on the basis of a wider
canvas than that of a narrow parochial view. Planning is a typical example. The
overall structure plan within a Metropolitan County needs this broad canvas if
there is not to be conflicting policies in adjoining areas, and if needless competition for industrial and commercial development at the ratepayers expense is to
be avoided. It is the implementation of these broader plans which needs to be
made at the lowest possible level. This operated very well in many pre-re-organis-
ation counties where the small district councils had considerable powers on minor,
but to the geographical area affected, important matters. It is of course impossible not to have conflict of opinion between two councils covering such activities
as planning. For example, the location of gipsy sites and refuse disposal tipping
facilities are matters which raise considerable local emotions, and no one can get
an accolade for making the necessary decisions on these matters! Such situations
call for considerable statesmanship. It is also an invaluable reminder to
councillors that while being elected by local wards they also have a wider
function to exercise, namely to the community as a whole. By and large, councillors
are able to achieve this and it works reasonably well.

When it comes to the Arts and Recreation, the cinderella of council activities,
problems arise for quite different reasons. When there are cutbacks in public
expenditure and one party is in control locally but in the minority at Westminster,
there is a tendency for dogmatism to overrule a commonsense approach to the expenditure of monies. This was clearly exhibited by the Conservative controlled G.M.C.
(1977-78) at a time of the Labour government in 1977-78. The edict to their own
supporters to cut public expenditure made by the Conservative shadow spokesman at
Westminster led to the dogmatic refusal of the local Conservatives at county level
to support the building of the National Ice Skating Rink, although one Conservative
council - Stockport - was willing to supply the land for a peppercorn rent!
Clearly the provision of such a facility is a regional and not a local matter.
A county authority such as the G.M.C. must accept a regional role in such matters
or it will be in dereliction of its duty. The argument put forward by the G.M.C.

was so narrow that it escaped its notice that other conurbations would gladly grasp this nettle to have such a national stadium, and would not accept, so meekly, the dictates of their national spokesman. When the county left it to the City of Manchester to press for such a scheme on its own behalf, the county authority exhibited a lack of forethought, in contrast to those Mancunian forebears who constructed the Manchester Ship Canal! It seems that the visionaries of yesteryear have few counterparts to-day. Yet the new counties are the nearest equivalent to the possible regional authorities of the future and require above all very perceptive councillors at the helm!

The ice skating rink is one example of the need for each of the two tiers in local government to recognise its role and to act accordingly. There are a number of leisure activities such as major theatrical productions, sports arenas, and events which have a much wider catchment area than that of the district in which they are situated. Of course, those nearest to the venues are likely to benefit most, but the proliferation of these facilities within each district is not yet feasible, let alone viable. Therefore, financial initiative by the county must be willingly given although it should always be open to the county to ask for and receive additional finance from one or more district councils appropriate for the venue(s). However, the wrangle over the City of Manchester's Art Gallery where an agreement was entered into by the City and County in the period of Labour control of the G.M.C. (1974-77), but was torn up when the Conservatives gained control, does little to commend the use of concurrent functions in this field. As stated earlier, this arrangement for concurrent function and agency agreements can only work if each accepts it's own responsibility and is prepared to discharge it effectively.

A number of authorities have endeavoured to set up schemes to counter-balance the centralising effect of the new authorities, by establishing local contact points by using the offices of the former constituent authorities. In Stockport they have established a number of Information Centres which provide an invaluable means whereby local people can seek information, register complaints, the elderly obtain bus passes, and numerous other services. In case of strikes involving refuse collection, residents used these information offices to pick up plastic bags for use. Some of the offices act as an outlet for Tourist Boards. The number of visits by the public are considerable, although still more people could make use of the facilities. There is, however, a clash between the county and the Stockport Borough over the use of Consumer Advice Centres which form part of the Consumer Protection Service of the county. Stockport is the only one of the ten districts within the G.M.C. which does not have such a centre run by the county.

In the county's search for premises, it appears to the onlooker that Stockport's insular attitude amounted almost to total opposition to the county's plan to establish an effective consumer advice service. The Stockport Borough refused to grant permission for the change of use from a shop to an advice centre, and then offered a totally inadequate alternative. It seems that some members and officers within the borough considered that such a centre was in direct competition with its own advice centres! This is a clear example of needless antagonism between district and county, which fundamentally arose out of a failure by the borough to understand the nature of the service provided by the county, and that service's relationship to the Office of Fair Trading. It is even more difficult to comprehend this situation when there are councillors who serve on both the county and district council. My own view is that these members not serving on the county's Public Protection Committee have either failed to understand or even to investigate the real nature of the service of consumer protection, or worst still, opposed the concept of consumer protection with its associated advice centres on grounds of political dogma.

The complex nature of commercial transactions, the use of advertising without guarantees of accuracy or performance, means that many members of the public are at the mercy of the less scrupulous traders. The consumer protection service not

only provides a service to help victims of unfair trading, but it does perform a
positive service to protect fair traders from unfair competition. Unfortunately
there are those who enshrine the doctrine of 'caveat emptor' in their political
philosophy. If those who take this view really understood the nature of the work
of these consumer advice centres, and their essential link with the national system
of introducing enforcement measures to root out undesirable practices, they would
not have been so ready to use the natural antagonism between county and district
to serve political ends. Such action indicates that many councils do not acknow-
ledge the tasks and duties entrusted to each authority.

It is worth recalling, when discussing the post-1974 organisation of local government that relationships between the tiers of government were influenced by strong
feelings of a parochialism which acted to the detriment of some ratepayers. This
is very true of education. Time and again where facilities did not exist within
the authority for special categories, such as children with special handicaps,
some authorities declined or were reluctant to pay 'out-county' fees for such
children to attend special schools run by other educational authorities.

Similarly, if a parent considered that one institution of higher education outside
his educational authority was best suited to his child, and possibly possessed a
reputation of a higher standard of which he wished to take advantage, there was
often a refusal to pay these 'out-county' fees on the grounds that the authority
has its own institution. Such attitudes by councils can be explained as being
due to the desire to keep their own institutions viable, but it does cast serious
doubts upon the 'professionalism' of many education administrators, by seemingly
placing administrative convenience as a higher priority than the quality of
education. Such an attitude fails to accept that standards do differ between
establishments. It tends to perpetuate indifferent standards and makes it expensive
to maintain mediocrity.

This conflict between authorities for educational facilities could well be intens-
ified once the predicted decline in pupil numbers reaches the stage of higher
education. As the metropolitan district is the educational authority, it could be
that if they cannot place the needs of their further and higher education students
as the first priority, there could be a strong case for removing higher education
from the metropolitan districts and placing it under the aegis of the metropolitan
counties, and so cut out the unnecessary duplication of resources. Those metropolitan districts which might be alarmed at such a suggestion are already planning to
set up sixth form colleges to cater for those problems which will shortly arise
when the fall in pupil numbers reaches the sixth form.

There are other areas where the boundary between county and district responsibilities can cause friction. The division of refuse collection from refuse disposal
has some merit in that the former is very much a local matter which can be visual-
ised by the ratepayer as being appropriate for the lower tier of government, and
the problems of finding scarce sites for disposal could be a problem needing a
solution on a wider scale than that of a metropolitan district council. Unfortunately this separation of the disposal facilities from the district discourages the
use of schemes designed to convert refuse into sources of energy, such as heat or
electricity for incorporation in district heating schemes or similar projects.
The failure to use refuse for positive purposes must surely be condemned as a needless waste of a possible resource. The fact that the development of viable altern-
atives can be hampered by the division of collection and disposal between two often
jealous tiers of government doesn't help to solve a national problem.

Whenever there are different tiers of government, whether national and local, or
even parish and district, there will always be some jealousy of the powers exercised by the senior partner with a desire of the senior to incorporate still more

within its control. It is the story of the gradual diminution of local power throughout the ages. Jealousy is not helped when powers are ill-defined or when the parties themselves do not respect each other's competence. When jealousy is coupled with an assumption that matters decided on a larger scale must be better in quality because of size, the situation is fraught with difficulty for the innocent ratepayer who while footing the bill wants a sensible answer, one which is appropriate to his needs, however parochial it may be.

There is therefore a tendency even with the establishment of the two tier system of local government for an unnecessary amount of fixed county or district-wide policies which take little account of local needs. When the planning authorities fight amongst themselves, when personal ambition of a senior officer leads to extension of his or her empire, particularly at the higher tier of government, there is a real danger of making local government even more remote than it need be. There is no easy solution because it depends upon the calibre of officer with complementary calibre of councillor. There is always the possibility that local government service will be seen as placing greater emphasis on the opportunity to provide employment, rather than to provide a public service. When such attitudes prevail, the relationship between the two tiers of government could well be conditioned by any attempt to seek personal aggrandisement through empire building.

There is so much within the new structure that depends upon relationships, therefore the success or otherwise of this aspect of local government depends ultimately upon the quality of those who serve local government, whether officer or member level. Ultimately the problem is not so much one of structure, but of human relationships of those involved at the point where the tasks and duties of the two tiers overlap.

CHAPTER 9

Management — Structure and Training or the Myth of Management

Local government has been a target for considerable criticism, especially since the reorganisation of 1974, when many small, intimate authorities became merged into the larger units with the administration problems associated with increased size. The task of managing such large departments as an experience new to a number of officers, and in consequence the gaps in managerial ability, techniques and procedures became exposed to the extent that far more people became aware of the shortcomings. There was, and still is, a grave danger of fitting a structure round people, rather than developing managerial skills so that they can operate within an optimum structure.

The most striking feature of local government is the predominance of professional men and women employed within the staff grades. In central government it is the administrators who are the key personnel exerting a very strong influence, which in some cases amounts to almost a stranglehold over professional staff. By professional, I mean qualified persons who are members of a professional institution. Anyone who followed the advent of Sir Donald Gibson and his professional team into the then Ministry of Works in the 1960s, and their subsequent submergence under the administrative steamroller will know what I mean. In local government it is the reverse, in that the administrator is subordinate to the professional.

My experience in the construction industry is that members of the professions have less training in management than any others within the construction team. Professional officers within local authorities are no exception. Seldom, if ever, is a management qualification specified as a requirement for any senior post. There is the most naive of all assumptions, namely that professional and technical skills carry with them a stamp of competence in handling resources and, in particular, in managing people and providing motivation. There is no promotion bar which can only be surmounted by a management qualification. It is the technological qualification satisfying a professional institution which seems to impress the interviewer. Little wonder, therefore, that management remains the neglected skill within local government.

There are a number of factors which indicate that management within local government has not developed very far. These include the inadequate comprehension of the concept of corporate management as exemplified by the very strong departmental independence, the failure to appreciate the difference between line tasks and service functions with the consequent inadequate organisation structures, the mental confusion in describing what are in effect Joint Negotiating Committees as Joint

Consultative Committees, the lack of any programme to develop staff, particularly through the use of delegation, the lack of any system for establishing managerial accountability, and the inability to comprehend the nature and function of job des- descriptions.

It is appropriate therefore to start with the structure of local government. Taking the duties entrusted to the metropolitan districts as the basis for discuss- ion, there are six activities which can be equated with the individual product lines of private enterprise. They are:

1. Social Services

2. Education

3. Housing

4. Highways

5. Environmental Health

6. Recreation and Culture

I shall refer to these activities as line tasks. A private business man might argue that these line tasks could be organised as if they were separate companies. Unlike manufacturing industry, these activities are very interdependent with the additional factor of a single source of finance, in contrast to the variety of sources available to separate companies within a group. In local government, various sections or persons within these line tasks can be called upon at times to provide a service function to a line task in another department. This happens when, for instance, certain social workers operate within the educational field, and when architects provide expertise for the education department. There are a number of basic service functions which should be readily available to those who undertake the above line tasks, namely, legal, administrative, personnel and estate management.

The particular structure adopted by an authority is indicative of the extent to which the corporate nature of a local authority's work is viewed by both officers and members. The former smaller authorities usually had a strong personality as the Town Clerk (or equivalent title) who knew most of the staff individually and could ensure that their activities dovetailed in together. It is the larger units which now require a structure as well as a procedure to establish true corporate management due to the interdependence of many activities.

It is feasible for the organisational structure to be influenced by the committee structure. There is always the dange of the 'tail wagging the dog'. The committee atructure can and has been in some instances tailored to suit the involvement of the elected members rather than to reflect the corporate nature of local govern- ment. The question of members' involvement has been dealt with in an earlier chapter, but it is appropriate to remind the reader of the possible interaction with the organisational structure of an authority when discussing the methods of organising local authority activities.

It is the failure of local government to appreciate fully the sharp distinction between line tasks and service functions which prevents a meaningful structure. There is the school of thought which supports the separate company approach common in private industry and which would incorporate the service functions within the departments responsible for line tasks, and by so doing retain the independence of departments associated with the traditional local authority approach. There is,

however, a serious warning needed for those who would advocate the continuation
of this system, that they will tend to destroy not only the career structure of
those qualified in the service activities, such as personnel, law, finance, etc.,
but also the basis upon which new entrants to these functions could be trained. If
all a local authority requires from these service activities is a series of
advisers, where is the corporate policy? Equally, it is possible that service
units could have inadequately qualified and experienced personnel within the line
departments. For example, one authority has unqualified personnel specialists in
certain departments. What is more alarming are assumptions by departmental chiefs
that the staff involved are professionally skilled!

The importance of the service functions must be fully appreciated, otherwise the
technical and procedural requirements may be inconsistent to the disadvantage of
the authority. Taking the personnel function as the example again, unless there is
a central personnel policy operative throughout the authority, there will be a wide
variety of policies, which in the case of industrial relations matters could be
utilised very astutely by employee groups and their representatives to set one
department off against another. One authority has deliberately exposed itself to
this situation but salvages its conscience by titling those personnel officers at
the centre as advisers. In consequence they act as a fire brigade whenever trouble
looms, seldom able to prepare plans to anticipate events. It is no wonder that the
gradings of staff in the various departments are unrelated and never subject to
effective scrutiny. Such a situation leads to chaos and can often be very expensive as departmental heads seek preferment for their own staff, regardless of the
total picture.

The supervision of safety is often placed within the umbrella of the personnel
function. The manner in which these safety duties are discharged can also be indicative of the corporate nature of an authority's management. It is clear to all
conversant with the Health and Safety at Work etc. Act 1974, that the chief executive is ultimately responsible for all safety matters within the authority. It is
a burden from which he cannot escape. This means that his remit must run throughout the whole organisation; yet such is the timidity of some chief executive
officers and the powerful influence of some departmental heads that his central
safety officer is often only an advisor!

If ever there was an opportunity to install an effective management control within
an authority and to indoctrinate otherwise reluctant departmental heads, it is presented by this Act in relation to safety matters, and it would enable the chief
executive to establish a strong safety policy and programme. I have found in my
studies that an authority's safety policy is the best indication of managerial
effectiveness from the top. What applies to the council as a whole, applies
equally to each department.

A strange twist in the relationship between line tasks and service function comes
about when a department, fulfilling its own line tasks, fails to appreciate its
own role relative to the service function it seeks from another section of the
authority. Many years ago when directing a major research project into the
'Structure and Economy of the Building Industry', we sought as part of that research
to identify the role played by client departments such as Education. In 90% of the
cases where we endeavoured to ascertain the client's design brief to the architects
in respect of schools, we were referred by the chief education officers direct to
the architectural departments. It appeared that the client/user function of establishing the design brief was passed over lock, stock and barrel to another department without any guidance, etc. In fact, it could well be contended that some of
the layouts of schools were decided without the teaching profession (and therefore
the user) being consulted. It leads many to wonder whether some of the designs of
modern schools are creatures of fashion rather than the result of carefully

researched and controlled educational experiments!

In such cases, the architects usurp the executive role of the client. They are, more often than not, closeted in another building away from those they serve with the result that there is a grave danger of inadequate interaction between designer and client. I contend strongly that designers of schools should 'live and eat' with the educationalists, this is the way to be fully responsive to the needs of their educational client. The shouts of horror at such a suggestion can be heard ringing through some of the architectural ivory towers! This is not to assert that architecture should become subservient to the educationalist. The lines of responsibility need to be changed from the traditional one to that of technical responsibility of the school architect to the chief architect (or whatever title), with a service responsibility to the client such as the education department.

Those designers who presume to know the client's mind should remember a hypothesis put forward by Mr. Stringer, late of the Tavistock Institute, when investigating the relationships within the construction industry that "the construction processes and the contractual arrangements are conducted in a manner that the interests of the client appear to be of little consequence"!

Many architects and others in a similar service situation will argue that it is a service which they seek to provide. Careful examination, however, reveals that the appreciation of these two different roles is misunderstood and often undeveloped. The worst disaster which can occur is where the client takes over responsibility for the technical service function. Another example is illustrated from my experience with one authority when each department was responsible for contract administration of its own building programme. In this instance, it was proposed to build three identical buildings in three different locations. Tenders were invited on the basis of three bills of quantity; one for a single building, another for the Preliminaries covering all three buildings, and the third for all the landscape work required on the three sites. When the tenders were opened it was decided to build two but not the third building. Yet a very inexperienced officer from the client department proposed that the contract should be placed on the basis of doubling the tender contained in the Bill for the single building plus the combined total of the Preliminaries and landscape bills. When it was pointed out to him that the last two bills should be proportional, since they covered three such buildings, his comment about the Preliminaries Bill was that "it didn't matter because they were only preliminary"! Those conversant with the construction industry will be excused if they have fallen about with laughter. For those not conversant with the construction industry, it should be explained that a Preliminaries Bill covers those services and items not directly connected with the physical measurements of construction work, but which incur costs that must be expended to give effect to a completed contract, such as supervision, plant, etc. This story illustrates the type of inadequate organisational structure liable to arise when the relationship between service function and line tasks is inadequately appreciated. Needless to say, when this defective organisational structure was exposed, the situation was duly remedied without even a committee meeting!

It is therefore important to set out the relationship between the line task and service functions. Dealing firstly with the purely service activities, such as personnel, legal, etc., it is desirable that members of the respective service groups should become fully conversant with particular line functions in much the same manner that committee clerks have always been assigned to particular committees. A decision must be made as to whether one person should serve one or more line tasks, or whether more than one is needed. This depends upon the workload involved which should be very carefully assessed. Once that is done, the director of the line task can rely upon the appropriate service functions being discharged within the central technical procedures laid down by the chief of that service function. The directors of these line tasks must accept that from time to time those in these service functions are moved to other duties to broaden their experience and knowledge so that they are better able, if found suitable, to take over the role required of central technical direction, and therefore better trained when they are appointed to fulfil a corporate function within the authority.

It may be noticed that I have excluded the development function (i.e. Design Services) from being classified as a line task. The reason for this is that development by a local authority never takes place for its own sake. There is always a client for whom the development is required, such as housing, education, etc. Even in the case of a joint development project between the council and private enterprise, there must be a brief prepared by a client who must ultimately carry the responsibility for the success or failure of the scheme. Those who are involved in the design services department do not carry this responsibility. Usually the development department is headed by an architect or engineer who exercises his role in his professional capacity, co-ordinating many of the services needed to give effect to the development. They are not 'developers' as such, who carry the responsibility beyond the physical construction.

I do not know of a joint venture where the authority has a role other than that of a financial shareholding, which extends the physical construction into the operational management of the completed scheme. If it did I would be a little concerned that a local authority could well be entering a field where it has little or no expertise. Where does this development role really come within the line task and service function areas? In 1966 I wrote an article on the 'Development of Cities' which was published in the journal "The Builder". Nothing has transpired since that date to alter the concept which I advocated, namely, the grouping together of the technical services associated with construction activity. This is now accepted practice in a number of authorities.

The basic concept arose out of the departmental independence and its effect on the redevelopment schemes associated with slum clearance. The interminable delays between the first acquisition of a property and the completion of a new dwelling on that site caused the timespan to extend often over a period of five to ten years. The basic reason was due to the lack of co-ordination between the various disciplines involved. Therefore no corporate management of the task of effecting re-development schemes existed. There was no committee structure to ensure that there was co-ordination between each departmental committee, for each jealously guarded its own empire and work programme without a real awareness of the effects of one upon the other. At this time the National Building Agency began to extend its consultancy work into the local authority field where it was involved in advising those authorities which recognised the need to establish co-ordination and control of all the activities involved in the development process. Whether the N.B.A. was timid in its approach, or succumbed to the existing constraints of local authorities as being too much for it, is a view which will depend upon the standpoint of the adjudicator. Nevertheless the task of co-ordination was often assigned to a deputy within the Town Clerk's department. Since the Town Clerk had no explicit brief whereby he was fully accountable for the totality of the Councils' operation, this appointment, particularly at a salary grade below that of the Chief Officers of the departments concerned, did not carry the weight which the duty merited and meant that the appointee had little effective control.

The appointment of Directors of Development, as I advocated back in 1966, was a welcome change in that there were attempts to provide at top tier level someone with responsibility in this field. Yet I have serious reservations about the system which has been adopted as it has not gone far enough in establishing a definite distinction between line tasks and service functions, because these officers in many instances are departmental heads of some, but not all, of the service functions needed for development purposes.

If a slum clearance scheme or a major development is proposed a number of specialists are needed to prepare the scheme in detail. These include:

Surveying

Legal

Planning

Civil Engineers

Architects

Other specialist designers

Quantity Surveyors

The statutory undertakings of water, gas, electricity and the Post Office could
also be involved in schemes. It could be a redevelopment scheme solely for housing,
or it could be a mixed development by including schools, industry, etc. The major
management duty therefore is to ensure that each phase in the process is planned
and completed in a manner that keeps delays to a minimum. It must be remembered
that the whole process is a very costly one. From the first acquisition money is
continually being spent and until the scheme is complete and rent and rates become
due, it is all outgoings without any revenue.

A wide variety of disciplines are involved in such schemes in differing degrees.
All these independent specialists need to be controlled and directed. This
requires management expertise of the highest order. After many years of association with the construction industry, I am convinced that these management functions
required for the development process need to be undertaken by persons who are not
involved in the day-to-day details of a professional discipline within the scheme.
It is clear from the above list of specialisms that a co-ordinator has to call upon
services from many departments if the task of Project Management, as I prefer to
call it, is to be successful. Above all, as I indicated earlier, professional
practices are not renowned for being amenable to the constraints imposed by management systems and techniques. Accordingly the requirement for someone to undertake
this task is paramount.

Not all schemes require intensive involvement of all the specialists. Even if
there is a simple scheme like a new Civic Theatre, there is a need for a project
manager to assist in establishing the design brief to meet the aims and objectives
of the client through which he can ensure that the requisite disciplines integrate
their own activities with those of others, once the decision to proceed is made.

For those who are not conversant with development projects it should be emphasised
that construction does not lend itself to rigid sequential processes of a number
of activities. At each of the various stages of development there is a greater
inter-dependency than many suppose, hence the need for rigid control and direction
to reduce delays which would arise if there was no integration of the disciplines
involved.

It is interesting to note that in the 60's there was a substantial atomic energy
programme under the aegis of the Atomic Energy Authority which established the role
of project manager undertaken by an officer of a complementary discipline to that
which undertook the key design activity. If it was a building where architecture
played the key role the Chief Engineer acted as project manager, while if

engineering was the major component as in power station construction, the chief
architect took this management role. The project manager should therefore be seen
as one who specialises in this management role. He should not compromise his
independent position as the manager by being professionally involved in the scheme.
Whether he is drawn from a particular discipline is immaterial. What is crucial is
his or her managerial capability.

If the Director of Development within an authority performs a similar role to that
of the project manager outlined above, he will cease to be responsible for the
individual service function of his discipline, such as architectural advice in
relation to educational, recreational and other projects. If he is placed at the
head of a limited group of professional disciplines, such as architecture or planning he may, due to the hierarchial structure of the authority, have no managerial
authority over the highway engineers, for example, who may be involved in a scheme,
especially if the highways engineers are headed up by a departmental head on the
same salary grade. There is therefore a case for making a Director of Development
the deputy of the Chief Executive with overall responsibilities for controlling all
types of project work. If this arrangement was made, the continuous saga of
financial expenditure planned for one year slipping into the next because of delays
through lack of managerial control may become the exception rather than the rule.

This approach to the management of development schemes reinforces my assertion that
the disciplines required for project work are regarded as providing a service
function rather than a line task since they serve the appropriate client - education, housing, environmental health, etc.

It is appropriate at this stage when project management is discussed to refer to
the part played by the central government. While a director of development may
have an effective control mechanism for ensuring co-ordination of the authority's
programme, an authority is always at the mercy of ministry approvals, planning
appeals, public inquiries, etc. The time taken to reach a decision is nothing less
than diabolical in some instances. There have been cases where confirmation of
Compulsory Purchase Orders, requests for relaxation of Building Regulations, and
the promulgation of decisions on appeals etc. have taken up to twelve months or
even longer. It is time that the Secretaries of State realised the effect of their
procrastination. It is not enough for Ministers to request that authorities make
a decision on a planning application within two months of submission if the appeal
procedure drags on for an inordinate length of time. No one likes seeing people
put their finger into a cash till, but there is little doubt that central government dips its fingers into 'the till of time'.

There is another aspect of the service function which is worth discussing before
leaving this topic. It is the role of an estates department. A close examination
will show that an estates department is mainly confined to the duties of acquisition and sale of council property. It is seldom concerned with estate management
as such, yet councils are often owners of vast estates. Admittedly the housing
authorities have specialist estate managers, or equivalent, within their respective
departments, but there is no corporate responsibility for estate management throughout an authority. Each department invariably regards the buildings within which
their activities take place as being their special domain! The educationalists are
past masters at this 'closed shop' concept of their schools, etc. The issue to be
faced is whether the authority is going to manage its property by qualified and
experienced estate managers, or to permit the non-expert to take over this duty.
leaving the estates department as a municipal estate agency business.

I hope that the lengthy discussion of my approach to the division between the line
task and service function and their inter-relationship will help the reader to
understand the need for a corporate approach to managing local government. The

corporate nature is established through the operation of the Management Board
comprising the chief officers (other titles are often used).

It is a fair criticism shared by a number of councillors of differing political
complexions that the management boards appear to be little else than policy cabals.
Seldom does a report from the management team contain managerial implications of
policy options or policy decisions of the council. More often than not, they are
a set of policy recommendations agreed amongst the officers which are presented as
a united front without the elected councillor having the benefit of hearing any
dissenting voice that may have been heard at the board meeting. It is as if there
is a doctrine of 'Collective cabinet responsibility' where a possible subsequent
disclosure of dissent is considered against the club rules! This is not to infer
that officers should not be able to assist in policy formation. They must be the
basic 'think tank' of the organisation working in parallel with the political
leaders. In fact I would go so far as to assert that elected members should attend
meetings of the management board, as advocated in Chapter 5. The reports of the
board should spell out the managerial consequences of various policy decisions.
Unfortunately there remains an attitude amongst certain officers which occasionally
borders on contempt as to the lay elected members potential contribution. This
attitude can have unfortunate consequences in certain situations where the policy
option and managerial implications are very intertwined. This is invariably the
case where the option involves a facet of reorganisation involving working methods
impinging upon industrial relations.

An example of this is a case where to effect reductions in expenditure, various
options are put forward in respect of refuse collecting systems. If the council
decides upon a preferred option before an agreement in the working arrangements is
made, the council could be held over an industrial relations barrel. If, on the
other hand, the industrial relations agreement is made before the council decides,
the 'tail wags the dog'. This is a case where the policy makers and the management
team have to work hand-in-hand. The members must clearly set out the objectives
to be achieved in the negotiations, bearing in mind the various policy options
available. This means that the leading members of the council must be members of
the negotiating body. The ultimate decision must be made by the council once they
are in possession of all the facts. The system therefore must be capable of achieving the council's objectives. It is the failure to do this which results in needless disruption of services to the public.

This is a typical illustration of the inter-dependence of policy and management
decisions. It also highlights the point made in the Bains report - New Local
Authorities, Management and Structure - of the dual nature of local government
management, which was discussed in Chapter 5 in respect of the role of councillors.

The concept of corporate management requires a suitable programme. This will be
referred to later when management training comes under the microscope.

A number of authorities seek to provide corporate management, yet councillors sometimes believe that having set up a management board, all management is corporate
thereafter! It is time for a real assessment of its operation in practice rather
than in theory. I have heard a comment by a junior member of the staff which may
be a fair reflection of opinion, that 'corporate management is left behind in the
boardroom once the chief officers have departed to their offices'. The lack of
training in corporate management is not the fault of various institutions offering
courses; it is a combination of councillor's reluctance in times of financial
stringency to spend money on training and in some cases combined with a reluctance
by chief officers themselves to go on courses. In one authority where a course
for departmental heads was arranged, they sent their deputies, presumably on the
grounds that good managers delegate! This attitude is a very poor reflection on

the understanding of management by officers. It does not inspire confidence that
other training courses will be purposefully used by their subordinates, or even
more important that they will select the right staff to attend courses.

Management is not only about people and organisations, it also concerns the use of
techniques, the collection of data and especially the use of statistics. In
Chapter 6 reference was made to the danger to which councillors can be exposed in
the presentation of statistics which may be meaningless. Councillors and officers
need to gain experience in the presentation and interpretation of data. Experience
has taught me, however, that as far as local government is concerned the form in
which statistics are presented and the use which is made of them becomes indicative
of the modus operandi of the authority. Similarly, it is another indicator of the
state of development of corporate management within local authorities.

Returning to the Area Digests prepared by the Corporate Planning Unit of Stockport
mentioned in Chapter 6, I do believe that there is a necessity for authorities to
step back and re-assess their true role within the community. The keynote is
service. They are not just another business which some officers and council employees appear to regard as a suitable place of employment. Their raison d'etre is
to serve the community, which means that it is fundamentally about 'people'. Therefore in presenting data for decision-making, one axis of the graph, or a factor in
a table, should be 'people'. Therefore for statistical presentation 'people' can
be classified in four major groups:

Age

Occupation

Economic groups

Social needs

It is the provision of services needed on a community basis which has to be viewed
from the standpoint of each of these groups. If this is done, an entirely different picture is presented of a local authority's tasks and performance. For
instance, instead of assessing where the schools and houses are, it would indicate
whether persons of under school age, school age, young persons, low income, retired,
disabled, handicapped etc., have the requisite provisions for education, leisure,
homes, special facilities, etc. The question of shortfall, or excess as the case
may be, can be more clearly identified, and the priorities as between conflicting
demands more easily established. It becomes a decision-making tool, rather than
the 'interesting' statistics as revealed in these particular digests. There is all
the difference in the world between 'interesting' statistics and 'useful' ones. It
is a pity that so many officers and councillors are sometimes unable to discern the
difference!

An illustration of this approach is provided by taking the age group 5 - 11 as an
example. The needs of this group include housing, education, recreation and
leisure pursuits. While the majority of this group will be housed with their families, there will be a proportion who are, (taking national averages) or could be
expected to be found, in the care of an authority. Everyone would hope that there
would be vacancies within the authority's provision for child care rather than
witness pressures for extension of them, but the balance between provision and
potential or evaluated demands is required for decision-making purposes. Equally,
when it comes to sporting facilities, the Digests listed the parks and playgrounds
with their associated facilities, but it omitted any mention of the acreage of
school playing fields, yet these are used by this age group! The reason for such
an omission was exposed when the officials were challenged on this matter. Their

reply was that these playing fields belonged to the Education Committee! How many members of the Education Committee has the reader seen playing on them? Another reply was that the head teacher would not let the fields be used other than in school hours. Yet such school playing fields are provided specifically for the use of children of that age group, and therefore effective use should be available outside school hours as well as during the school term. Many children are barred from such facilities, particularly in the holidays, by this traditional approach. This reaction by the establishment is typical of the insular departmentalism of so many local authorities, which as stated earlier, reflects both their attitudes and their organisational structure.

The reader must be informed, however, that reforms are on the way, thank goodness, albeit very slowly and only after personnel retire or move on! In Stockport the maintenance of school fields is vested in the Recreation Division, but it has little control over their use, except where special arrangements have been made for organised groups to use them out of school hours and during the holidays. This is a step in the right direction. But it is four years and more since the departmental attitude set out in the digests was challenged in my memorandum to the Director of Administration.

Local government still has a very long way to go to change its philosophy and attitude towards its ratepayers so that 'people' become the overriding priority rather than the 'system'.

Managers have to use statistics and councillors like directors need them to make their policy decisions. But as long as local government fails to produce meaningful statistics for decision-making purposes, the less ably will it fulfil its task of serving the community and its needs. In order that the reader may be aware of the approach which I consider appropriate, I set out extracts of the memorandum I submitted. "The Borough is the corporate guardian of all its citizens". "The Borough consists of *people*, without *people* there would be no Borough. Let us look at the problem and needs of the Borough *through the eyes of people* and not through its buildings, services, or any other media, for such are the servants, the aids, by which *people* live in the fullest meaning of the term."

Probably the most serious of all of management's failings is the lack of positive action to provide motivation and job satisfaction in many areas. This is due to the attitude which places greater emphasis on systems and procedures than on peoples' capabilities and responsibilities. When Walter Bagehot wrote his treatise on the Constitution he referred to checks and balances. In local government the emphasis as far as an individual's contribution is concerned suffers from excessive checks! This is not to pour scorn on those authorities which have established extensive delegated powers to officers. Where there are powers delegated to the officers by the council, the procedure for reporting back on the use of these powers is sometimes cursory or non-existent. In some cases, the officers have power to effect improved gradings of their staff, yet I have heard of instances where departmental heads have re-graded (upwards of course) staff even when the Personnel Officer has advised against such a course! Without a reporting-back procedure the councillors remain in the dark as to management's action, but are expected to endorse at budget time the consequential bill! Infortunately, even when revised staffing proposals or staffing reviews take place, the new grade can be taken as the base, rather than the original grade which was determined by the appropriate committee.

I did find an effective and regular reporting-back system when I served on the Greater Manchester Council. It enabled councillors not only to be acquainted with use of the delegated powers, but also to ask pertinent questions. It is therefore worth reminding councillors that when management delegates, management does not

absolve itself from the responsibility for the way those delegated powers are used.
In the event of abuse it may indicate that it was wrong to grant such delegation
in the first instance, or that the person to whom the powers were delegated is
unsuited to the task. This is what true accountability is about, and councillors
cannot abrogate their responsibilities in this matter, however much they might wish
to search for scapegoats! There is an apparent reluctance among chief officers to
delegate. It is traditional in a number of departments that the head of it insists
that all correspondence is addressed to him; yet in the corner of letters dispatch-
ed from him, it states "please contact M/S X etc.", but woe betide a member of the
public, let alone a councillor, who contacts M/S X direct by letter, although
verbal communication direct is not frowned upon! One head of department, when
questioned about the identity of the person who performs the personnel function
within the department, stated that he did! Yet to the best of my knowledge this
same head has not received any training in the personnel management function.
Presumably he assumed that training and experience in personnel matters is superfluous. Does he recruit all the staff, write all the job specifications, interview
all employees, etc.? Does he really comprehend the nature of delegation, has he
had any training in management skills, or was it another case of learning through
"sitting beside Nelly"?

A reluctance to delegate could arise from a fear that the subordinate might make a
mistake in the exercise of his judgement. If this is the case, it is possible for
the organisation to become ossified, morale drop, and in the end the quality of
subordinate will fall below that commensurate with remuneration. Unfortunately,
the ratepayers become the chief sufferers and the task of pulling the organisation
out of its slough of despond takes considerable time.

It would be worth drawing the attention of such officers who exhibit a reluctance
to delegate that it would not be unreasonable for their subordinates to receive
the impression that they are not to be trusted. Frustration caused in this way
could be a cause of the increasing use of leaks to the press! Ultimately the
chief officers as much as councillors have to realise that the effectiveness and
efficiency of an organisation depends more upon the quality of the staff at all
levels, and not of the system employed. This means accepting that each and every
one of us is in a continuous training situation, where experience is gained even
through errors, and we must expect that there will be mistakes from time to time.
But to build up a procedure to prevent any mistakes at all stultifies any personnel
development and turns the staff into robots.

I have always found a reluctance by the chief officers to delegate to their own
staff the duty of reporting to a committee on those reports which their staff have
prepared. Each chief officer reserves this to himself, believing correctly that
he is ultimately responsible. Yet it is not uncommon to find that he is often not
fully conversant with all the details which went into the preparation of the report.
I have known many junior officers feel a sense of frustration when they hear reports
of how their chiefs have handled the matter at the committee meeting. Equally, I
have found reports being given at one committee by one officer being totally con-
tradicted by another officer at another, simply because one of them has not turned
up the record of events, or worse still because discussions, etc. have never been
recorded and put on the file. It may be that chief officers do not delegate this
task of reporting to committees because they desire to protect subordinates. As a
matter of principle, I believe that this attitude is misguided. I cannot accept
the almost unconscious feeling among some chief officers that it is beneath their
dignity to allow a junior to present a report on a matter under their control. I
feel strongly that juniors should, after discussing their report with their chief,
be able to present the reports themselves with their chief as back-up facility.
There is nothing wrong in making juniors feel important and that they have an
important task to fulfil. It makes for a more effective department, and increases

job satisfaction. Treat juniors as paid hacks, and that is what they will become
if the present arrangements persist. It appears that too few chief officers have
learned this elementary lesson in the training of staff.

It is important to stress the part that delegation plays in providing motivation to
staff; it also provides one of the best methods of effecting on-the-job training.
However, this is not the place to write a training manual for the benefit of chief
officers and others, but it is the appropriate place to draw attention to those
areas where action is needed to enable local government to be both manageable and
effective. It is worth reminding officers and councillors alike that the
"achievements of any organisation can never exceed the expectations of the person
with the greatest power". This applies in the political as well as in the managerial field. It places a heavy responsibility upon those with the greatest power to
disseminate those expectations in order that the achievements may match them.

There is a fundamental difference between consultation and negotiation. Yet local
authorities act as if the words are interchangeable. They call what are in effect
negotiation committees Joint Consultative Committees; whether this is due to a
lack of appreciation of the science of management is difficult to assess. It
would be unfortunate if the confusion prevented real consultation. My limited
research indicates that few authorities have any formalised consultation within
the paid service.

Regulations under the Health and Safety at Work etc. Act 1974 provide for safety
representatives and safety committees. Some authorities are proposing, at the
unions' request, to set up joint committees of members and employees, yet the
officers and senior councillors appear to be treating such committees as negotiating committees! If ever there was a case for not negotiating at all, it is on
safety matters! To reinforce the negotiation aspect of these committees no doubt
they will have equal representation from each side!

Consultation requires that the person who has the power to make decisions or to
frame management programmes should be present. Consultation should concern itself
about the organisation's objectives, methods, and how they are implemented, as well
as informing management of the views of their employees on such proposals. In
consequence there is no need for a vote at such meetings, management should be in
a position to answer authoritatively any questions put by employees. Consultation
does not call for the 'sense of equality of representation' necessary in a
negotiation situation.

If therefore local government has the role of consultative committees so wrong in
concept, it is difficult to see whether it will ever be able to extricate itself
from this impasse and achieve effective consultation within a department or section.
That consultation is needed, I do not question. Few in senior management positions
are able to accept that the administrative process, policies and procedures, can
cause substantial aggravation. If full consultation comes about, where time,
effort and thought is needed by those who set the objectives, there is little doubt
that the frequent changes in procedures, etc. which occur in some authorities,
would almost disappear. It is often the arrogance of some managers which assumes
that others have no contribution to make. As time goes by, these managers will be
left behind in the wake of changing managerial thought and styles. The sooner some
of them disappear, the sooner another barrier to motivation will be brought down.

It will be clear from the description of the conduct of local government to-day
that there is an urgent need for action to be taken to provide some basic
managerial training. Like all such training, it should start at the top!

A number of chief executives have reached their present post without any formal

management training or an opportunity to study and develop in a training situation
the skills of corporate management. It is clear that the lack of training and exposure to many developments in management theory and practice will not be made good
if it is left to the whim of chief executives and other chief officers who head up
departments. It may well be essential for the central government to intervene.
This will require powers to enable selection or short-listing for senior posts to
be subject to the approval of a Minister in much the same way that the Home Secretary has to approve certain appointments in the Police and Fire Services. This
would be a drastic step and one which would no doubt be sincerely resisted by many
councillors and very probably officers as well. But both councillors and officers
will have only themselves to blame if severally and jointly they fail to act to
ensure that adequate management training is provided.

It is clear that if chief executive officers are required to undergo training, then
it is pointless to leave it until they reach this pinnacle of their career. There
is a basic need to start management training at a much lower level in the organisational hierarchy. I firmly believe that no one should be allowed to be appointed
to a post in the third tier of any department unless he or she has satisfactorily
completed a management training course. Thereafter, there will be a need to top-
up existing skills with an extension of training to fit him for a new post.

The only way this can be achieved is to ensure that staff have a right to elect to
undertake management training after a specified period in a post. I am disturbed
by the reluctance of councillors to finance management training as much as I am
concerned that officers concentrate training solely on the professional field. I
am aware that some councillors assume that senior officers must be able to manage,
otherwise they would not have reached their particular post! It is only when you
interview officers at this level, as I have done, that you find the appalling gaps
in their development of management skills for the post they seek. To those
councillors who would use financial restrictions as a defence for the present system I would urge them to tot up the present cost of managerial incompetence! A word
of caution is needed to those who set-up management training schemes; it would be
all too easy to set up a series of in-house training courses for management. It
can be a useful exercise, but total reliance on in-house provision would bring
about a form of 'managerial incest' at times when it is evident that a wind of
change is needed to blow through the hallowed walls of the Town and County Halls!
The importance of external exposure increases the more senior the post involved.

For some years I have been associated with the Diploma in Management Studies programme in the north of England. Basically it is a very sound development and has
tremendous potential in preparing local government staff for managerial posts, but
all too often it is only the very junior staff whom department heads are prepared
to release. A number of centres provide courses specially designed for the public
sector and local government should support more of them. I am concerned at the
attitude towards them because many students face difficulties in being allocated a
suitable project by their own authority for investigation and report. My impression is that some local authorities show greater resistance to these courses than
do many private firms who, in the case of project work, have commercial confidences
to be taken into account. Such reluctance confirms my impression of local government managerial standards. The European experience of Professor Revans in organising active project work in which students undertake projects in companies other
than their own, is a development which local government could well emulate.

Another disturbing feature of management within local government is manpower planning. There appears to be no positive forecasting of retirements and possible
succession, let alone identifying candidates for possible promotion and the
requisite training programme. In addition there appear to be few programmes designed to improve specialist skills by the use of new methods and techniques. Some

forethought on this matter is both desirable, feasible and of immediate necessity.

If there is not a potential successor amongst the junior posts, there is something radically wrong with the selection for the junior posts. This is not to advocate the restriction of appointments to those within an authority since any organisation benefits from an injection of new blood every now and then, but there should be at least a strong internal candidate. In some cases, some officers should be deliberately encouraged to seek posts elsewhere to broaden their experience, with a view to possible selection for a senior post in their present authority at a later date. To put it plainly, there needs to be some gumption injected into local government manpower planning. In answer to those who would complain about other authorities poaching trained personnel, if there was a basic right to elect for management training, the danger of one authority being the training ground for others would disappear. But there can be a substantial gain from being an acknowledged training ground; a department whose staff regularly are picked for senior posts in others, attracts recruits of a much higher calibre than those authorities where the post is little more than a resting ground or a stop-gap till the receipt of the old-age pension. The fact that personnel do not stay forever in the post selected must be acknowledged by the appointing committee (whether it is of officers or councillors). The worst offenders, I fear, are the councillors who assume that each appointment is for life! Some show a distinct reluctance to appoint if they suspect that the candidate will move on. If such behaviour exists, the chances of appointing the second best is greatly increased, to the detriment of the authority. However, when committees do appoint with a view to promotion, and I have had the privilege of being a member of such a committee which did this in the face of some opposition, then progress is being made in establishing some concept of career development from which the authority might benefit considerably.

Very seldom is there a report given to the appropriate committee of the training undertaken by the staff. It is very popular to go to Institution or Professional conferences and possibly to listen to various papers! Very few of these conferences ever provide sufficient time for the audience to assimilate the full implications of any idea or technique to debate or to ask questions in depth. Sometimes attendance at conferences is seen as the 'perks' of the post, yet it is probably the only time such officers are ever exposed to developments. All officers read their professional journals, but the benefit of knowledge acquired from debate seldom if ever percolates through into positive action by the council. Some authorities also provide information to members on the various articles available. I have used this service quite extensively, but the quality of the articles in many cases leaves too much to be desired, so that the benefits of this service is often minimal.

It is clear that experimentation and development should be a standard practice in all authorities. Some are nationally renowned for this activity, but the time scale of emulation by others is extended more into decades rather than years. In Chapter 10 I refer to the problem found in evaluating the priorities for different highway schemes. Yet research and development is going on outside local authorities into new techniques of evaluation, but few authorities are seen to use this research work, let alone commission others to carry it out on their behalf by those who study in this field. Once again the insularity of local authorities sticks out like a sore thumb. It is worth reminding the reader that when it comes to training, education departments do provide in-service training for teachers, judging by the number of days when schools are closed during term-time! Whether all teachers in a school which is closed attend a course on all or some of these days is not revealed to the public. Yet credit should be given at least to the attempt to plan such training!

I have had discussions with the Royal Institute of Public Administration which I would expect to lead in the field of management training, but information on suitable courses is scarce even from Henley staff college. The use of L.A.M.S.A.C. and the Industrial Training Board may have blunted all effective training other than for manual workers. The Institute of Local Government at Birmingham University has not made a great impact upon the scene. It is probably true to say that the whole area of management training within local authorities is the most neglected within the nation.

CHAPTER 10

Project Planning or the Confidence Trick

Every council has the task of planning a number of projects. These can range from large scale joint commercial or industrial developments to those for building and civil engineering projects. Each requires a different emphasis and grouping of skills and each has special characteristics demanding different treatment. The crucial aspect is the need for an effective overall management from conception through to completion. It is lacking particularly at the early stages, and this applies not only to the public sector but also to private industry. Professionals, and especially designers, are notably reluctant to submit themselves to managerial discipline. Since the management function has been discussed in Chapter 9, it will not be repeated here, but the contribution it makes to the various types of development which an authority undertakes is discussed.

Setting Priorities for Projects

There is a fundamental need for a sound basis for assessing the priorities in terms of resources for projects in the public sector. Although the financial accounting procedures directs the attention of the authority to the provision of finance to implement schemes, it is inevitable that the financial provision relates to the physical development work. There is a total absence of any consideration about the priorities needed to allocate resources to the initial phases of design and other preliminary work. Yet the resources within local government needed for design work, etc., are limited and can only be augmented by either engaging consultants or by approving additional appointments. If the limited resources of those in post are to be used effectively it is vital that priorities are determined as to their use. However, costings of this preliminary work are not prepared and submitted to councillors. Such costs are simply lost in the general salary provision and included in the running costs of the respective departments. The only way some assessment of costs of this preliminary work ever comes to light is when outside consultants are employed. If priorities were established by the councillors for the design work as well as for the physical construction, much of the present abortive design work would be avoided. It is all very well for the engineers reporting to committee to state that they need a library of highway schemes to pull out of the drawer whenever necessary, or to fill in the expenditure gaps at the financial year end, when there is no report as to which schemes within the library are being dealt with or have completed designs ready for implementation. If the true facts were revealed, the councillors let alone the ratepayers would be amazed.

In order to give some idea of the extent of this misuse of resources, it should be

recalled that in Greater Manchester Council's area alone at the time of reorganisation, there were over four hundred and fifty schemes resulting from the S.E.L.N.E.C.
(South East Lancashire & North East Cheshire) Transportation Plan. These schemes
in 1974 totalled nearly one thousand million pounds and at the then rate of construction would not be completed in the lifetime of any of the present population!

It should be stated that many schemes were simply lines on a map. However, a substantial number were at various stages of the design process. I never obtained a
satisfactory answer to my queries as to the state of readiness of these schemes,
but when a particular scheme came up for consideration there was always the assertion of the need to re-design it or re-appraise it in the light of changing criteria.
It was a standard excuse it seemed. As a result the council was kept in the dark
as to the true state of this preliminary work. Central government authorisation
concerns the physical preparation work, such as land acquisition, etc. and the
actual construction work, and it is only when this stage of the process takes place
that there is some public knowledge as to the state of readiness of the particular
scheme(s) involved.

The situation existing as the nineteen seventies draw to a conclusion is that there
is a very substantial amount of design work lying in office drawers awaiting the
light of day. This represents a serious mismanagement of scarce design manpower
as well as the financial resources needed to maintain these design teams. Local
authorities are not the only guilty ones. A colleague of mine recalls working on
the design of a new library extension for the University of Manchester way back in
the early nineteen sixties; now nearly eighteen years later the work on the site
has now started.

The reluctance of councillors to establish priorities for design work could well be
due to the fact that this means making decisions about matters which they may not
see fulfilled in their period of office. A councillor likes to have achievements
under his belt when seeking re-election. The public is often sceptical about prom-
ises of things to come. They have been disappointed too often. It is only when
work really starts that they will believe that the scheme has a chance of completion.

Whatever pressures exist, there is no excuse for councillors not being willing to
make decisions, the results of which may only be evident five to ten years hence.
That it is their duty to be involved at setting priorities for design work to be
undertaken by the council's staff, I have not the slightest doubt.

The revised system by central government for approving transportation schemes
introduced at the time of local government reorganisation is known as the Transportation Policies and Programme (T.P.P.). The system makes it possible for councillors
to have a greater control over the use of design resources. The T.P.P. system
enables transportation plans of every kind to be formulated for an immediate five
year rolling programme with an appropriate assessment of the expenditure beyond
the five year period, due to the starts in the latter part of the five year programme being carried beyond into the sixth and subsequent years.

While the central government makes grants available on an annual basis, there is on
the face of it an acceptance of the T.P.P. submission for expenditure in years
other than the year for which immediate grant approval is given. However, a close
examination of the submission will reveal that it is concerned with monies which
have to apply to the physical activities, such as land acquisition and construction
work. Design costs are not included, the presumption being that all schemes within
the T.P.P. have been designed ready for land acquisition etc. The creation of a
five year rolling programme does give a council an opportunity to establish its
priorities for the schemes, at least as far as physical work is concerned, and is
a welcome advance on previous systems.

It is only a relatively small step to remove the decision on priorities back to the design stage. Clearly all schemes which are included in the third and subsequent years of the T.P.P. submission should have been the subject of a cost benefit study to establish their priority for inclusion in the submission, and the two years prior to their anticipated starting date should be used for designing the appropriate details. In such cases the councillors will be setting their own priorities for design work. It will be contended that this is precisely what occurs, yet there is no assurance that other design activity on work not yet included in the fifth year of the programme is not being undertaken!

It was only in 1978 that the officers of the Greater Manchester Council submitted to the council their basis for selecting transportation schemes. However, they are using their selection procedures, not to establish priorities for inclusion in the T.P.P., but for the purpose of weeding out highway schemes from the original list derived from the S.E.L.N.E.C. Transportation Plan.

The purpose of this exercise should be explained. Once there are lines on a map there is an immediate danger of creating planning blight. Planning blight can prevent the sale of properties, halt improvements and lead to the degeneration of the environment in the area covered by the projected schemes. To understand the scale of the problem, a typical example is that prior to reorganisation, the City of Manchester instituted the process to acquire properties along the route of one of the schemes in this 'Grand Design' of the S.E.L.N.E.C. plan. Subsequently, it was clear that finance for this road would not be available because it ranked very low in the scale of priorities and was unlikely to be built within fifteen years at least. Yet one property so acquired was valued at some £11,000, but because the procedures had been initiated the owners demanded their right under the law to a new building on a new site. The cost of this in 1976-7 would have been approximately £½m. Such is the cost of unco-ordinated action and of the failure to inject management control into the whole process of highway planning. In order to relieve the excessive blight the Greater Manchester Council is slowly removing a large number of schemes put forward in the S.E.L.N.E.C. proposals, with the hope that it will be left with a list of schemes which, within the existing levels of resources, could be started within a fifteen year period besides removing blight from the rest of the schemes.

The Greater Manchester Council has finally decided to use an Operational Research method based upon certain criteria to determine the priorities of various schemes. They are:-

Criteria	based on
1. Overloading carriage-ways	Peak off-time traffic, and capacity of the carriageway.
2. Delays to buses	Number of buses, peak and off peak.
3. Delays to medium and heavy goods vehicles	Number of such vehicles peak and off peak. Delay in minutes.
4. Delays to other traffic	Numbers of vehicles, peak and off peak. Delay in minutes.
5. Environment and housing	Number of houses fronting, total traffic flows.
6. Environment - shopping	Shopping frontage, total traffic flow.
7. Pedestrian	Number of footways crossing road. Time waiting to cross capacity.
8. Accidents	The number of accidents in which people are injured.
9. Industry a. existing b. potential	Number of existing and potential jobs.

Taking each criteria separately, 100 points are given to the worst possible situation and then in descending order in proportion to the extent of the problem revealed by the measure used. This is a well-known technique used in industry. But a close examination has to be made not only of the criteria themselves or those items which are included, but also of the effect of the measure used to establish the proposed priority of the schemes.

Firstly, the use of the indicators for delays to medium and heavy goods vehicles bears a close relationship to the delays to other classifications of traffic. A close study of the figures given by the G.M.C. indicates that there is such a close relationship and that this indicator cannot be treated as a truly independent variable when used in conjunction with other indicators. To obtain the requisite list of priorities the score for each scheme given by each of the criteria is aggregated. If therefore the variables are not independent as indicated, then there is a form of double counting. What is more serious is the inherent bias in favour of vehicle traffic usage as against other road users.

Secondly, the problems faced by cyclists are ignored. This is a serious omission since it is possible that the inadequacy of suitable provision for this legitimate road user could be a major contributor to a higher accident rate than would be the case if their needs were catered for in the planning of highway schemes.

Lastly, there is a different effect upon the performance indicators in the case of road improvements as opposed to the building of new roads. The major changes in road usage which will occur after improvements will be the effect on traffic delays. However, new schemes will change traffic patterns on existing routes and the score should be enhanced by measuring the relief given to the existing routes

less the effect of possible attraction of additional traffic. To illustrate this,
the construction of the M63 to Cheadle Heath made it more beneficial to a number of
workers to use their cars to reach Trafford Park in place of the former use of the
nearest rail link, besides expected relief of a number of roads.

The system used by the G.M.C. is based on benefits alleged to accrue, there was no
associated cost included to derive a cost benefit comparison. At present, the
engineers have decided - not the councillors - that each of the criteria should
carry equal weight. The engineers see their own solution as being related solely
to the task of engineering traffic movement. It must be a matter for the politicians as representatives of the community to decide whether any or some of the
criteria should be given extra weighting in obtaining the final score. This is a
matter which must not be left to the professionals. It would be perfectly reasonable for the politicians to argue that the quality of life for the residents of the
neighbourhood of a particular road scheme should be given extra weight compared
with the effect of delays to other traffic. For instance, it is possible that
speed generated by improvements could isolate each side of an improved road and be
a disadvantage to the scheme on environmental grounds.

At present, the scheme adds all the scores due to the current problems a particular
road generates, but there is no subtraction from the score of the disadvantage as
suggested above which could detract from the desirability of a particular scheme.
The reader should be reminded that the fixing of a score using known data enables
a judgement to be made on historical data. Unfortunately, history is not a reliable
guide to the future especially when planners have future developments in mind. It
is not enough to consider these schemes on a short-term basis. If there are developments planned, particularly when they are for industrial estates, it could well
be that these schemes themselves become traffic generators especially if warehous-
ing is predominant. The heavy traffic such schemes generate is often very detri-
mental if the convenient routes to and from them encourage hauliers to use what
were predominantly residential areas.

The system of calculating benefits to traffic movements needs to be taken into
account when choosing the best area in which to site new industry and industrial
processes.

There is a role to be played by the politicians as suggested earlier, namely of
deciding on any weighting to be given to certain criteria the traffic engineers use.
Without the use of this system of establishing priorities for transportation schemes
there will always be opportunities for politicians to make special pleading for
their own pet schemes without the need to establish an overall judgement of the
relative merits. Politicians should not be disturbed by the crude nature of the
scoring process, as more data becomes available refinements can take place and the
resultant score move from the highly subjective to a more objective assessment.

One of the great advantages of the system is the fact that it concentrates the mind
on the totality of the problem and must ultimately improve the quality of the
decision making. Officers may argue that the whole process is best left to them,
but traffic engineers are no more blessed with superior crystal balls than any
other person. Their task is to improve the quality of the data to be used, and to
leave the politicians to make those decisions which reflect the community's priorities.

It is worth emphasising, before leaving this topic, that the Greater Manchester
Council did not devise this scoring system to select the schemes for inclusion in
the T.P.P. submission to the government - it is to be hoped that it will be used
for this purpose soon - but for the purpose of eliminating those schemes which they
inherited from the S.E.L.N.E.C. plan, and which cannot be reasonably foreseen as

being included within the next fifteen years. In this way considerable planning
blight which has generated considerable slum-like areas as explained earlier will
be removed. At the time when this operational research technique was revealed to
the Council, the process of elimination had reached phase four of the target of
reducing the number of schemes to those possible for completion within a fifteen
year period.

This phase had a total of 69 schemes listed, but eight of them had no score allocated, yet only one of these was included in the 19 recommended for elimination!
The points score ranged from 19 to 547. Of the 18 recommended for abandonment
which had scores, the highest score to be included in the list had 142, but the
range up to 142 contained a list of 30 schemes. The immediate question arises as
to why 12 schemes within this band were not included in the recommendation for
abandonment? There was no satisfactory explanation in the report other than that
they were retained for further review! If the criteria set out were admitted to
be inadequate, steps should have been taken to rectify the situation before making
decisions on data admitted to be inappropriate.

The whole purpose of using this operational research method is to provide greater
objectivity. If those schemes with the lowest scores are not included in recommendations for elimination it opens the door to special pleadings - often on emotional
grounds - and above all, destroys the whole purpose of using these techniques.

The above method of assessing priorities for transportation schemes has been discussed at length to demonstrate that it is possible to use scientific methods to
provide the decision makes with criteria upon which to base their decisions.
Further, it demonstrates that it is feasible to do this work before detailed design
work is started, and therefore it is possible to achieve a better utilisation of
the manpower and financial resources. It is a vast improvement on the former
system when a vocal pressure group, with the possible additional use of vested
interest pressure groupings, determined priorities. The fact that the system is
still in what I describe as a lower sixth form stage of development, should not be
used to condemn the attempts which are being made and the necessary awareness of
many officers of the need to develop these techniques still further.

Government and Project Planning

It is worthwhile looking more closely at the relationship between central and local
government on highway matters, since reorganisation of local government has enabled
central government to revise the scheme for approving expenditure on transportation
schemes through the T.P.P. system.

Prior to April 1975 there were five separate sources of funds:

a. Principal road grants

b. Public transport infra-structure grants

c. Rural bus and ferry grants

d. Grants to passenger transport executives towards the costs of rail passenger
    services, and

c. Specific contribution to expenditure on transportation studies

In revising the scheme into the single T.P.P. system the Secretary of State still
retained powers under certain statutes to pay other grants in exceptional circumstances.

As is usual with central government, it sets out to do one thing and then back-tracks. It stated: "one of the objectives of the new grant system is to avoid the need for detailed examination by the department of individual schemes" (para. 9 Department of Environment circular 27/74), and then modifies it by saying "In the early years however, when there will be limited experience of evaluating transport proposals in this strategic way, regional officers may need to discuss the justification .... etc. (para. 10 D. of E. circular 27/74)

It will be seen, therefore, that the purpose of the new system is to enable the transportation authority to look very carefully at all aspects of both public and private sectors and to integrate them into a strategic plan. This system can be viewed as being a conscious effort on the part of central government to move the decision-making area towards local government and the elected representatives. The snag comes, however, in the form of the role of the regional offices of the central government departments.

The role of the regional office first became clear to me when the transportation plan for rail services in Manchester included a proposal to integrate and up-grade the rail services within the conurbation which lacked a satisfactory connection between the two systems; the old London Midland operating out of Piccadilly Station mainly to the south, and the old Lancashire and Yorkshire lines from Victoria Station to the north. The proposal also included a distribution system within the city between these two stations. The transport executive had done the most extensive study ever and had submitted considerable data in support of its proposals. Once the data had been provided to the regional office of the ministry the latter went to work scrutinising all the data supplied. The delays were inevitable and almost interminable. At one meeting where the minister was present, a regional officer stated that it would be a considerable time before the checks would be complete and further that the office was still awaiting details; yet invéstigation revealed that this information had been supplied four months previously. Either they had not got down to it in their 'In Tray', or they were using, what many people experienced in local government believe, the traditional method of justifying delays!

It must be stated that this transportation plan, known locally as the Picc-Vic scheme, was prepared and submitted before the T.P.P. system became operative, but d due to the lapse of time it had eventually to be incorporated within the T.P.P. submission, since it was part of the overall transportation strategy of the county. Approval was not forthcoming. The Regional office could always hide behind the T.P.P. system which did not permit grants to be made available for such special items unless the regional office was in support. Time and again these officials said that there were either defects in the cost benefit analysis or something else was missing. Yet schemes like the Tyne Metro and the Fleet line in London could go ahead without such back-up material!

To try to go over the heads of the regional office and expect the minister responsible to make the final decision was unlikely to succeed, as the regional officials could lobby the Secretary of State at the Department of the Environment under whose wing the Transport Minister worked! It would need two strong personalities as the Transport Minister and the Secretary of State needed to be in accord to overrule the civil servants. Further, any attempt to seek outside financial support from the E.E.C., for example, requires government approval as well, so the chances of success were diminished. All the time there was a serious doubt about the ability of the regional office of the D. of E. to be flexible in its approach to the transportation problem of the conurbation, and to present the councils' proposals fairly to their superiors in Whitehall. This suspicion was heightened by the known former association of these officers with the development of the highway network in Glasgow. In consequence they were suspected of being unsympathetic towards the development of other transportation solutions, especially railways, with the legacy of the Beeching era still very dominant in transportation thinking. It was also possible that inexperience of railway development leads engineers to be dubious of its benefits!

It was clear that in certain circumstances the local authorities found themselves less free than the circular 27/74 implies, to plan and implement schemes. Later in 1976 there appeared to be some baulking of individual proposals and a meeting of representatives of the council and the regional office took place. It soon became clear that the senior staff of the D. of E. were exceedingly ill-prepared and were unaware of details of the schemes which had been supplied to their office. It was one occasion when the Leader of the Council became so infuriated with the situation that at one point he suggested abandoning the meeting and making direct representations to the minister concerned. Only after this threat was any reaction obtained; the civil servants scurried with their papers back to their office with a plea to meet again at a later date!

It must be appreciated that the regional staff of a ministry enjoy considerable independence and are also highly influential. Every step, and it is hoped that there will be more in future, to devolve decision-making down to local authorities will be met with very mixed feelings by regional officers who seem to have a delight in being free from the democratic accountability by endeavouring to make decisions themselves. Few like to lose powers, but it seems regional officers are more human than most!

Other forms of Project Planning

Every authority has other capital schemes than those involving transportation. Most involve construction activity of some kind. While the effectiveness of the final solution will depend in some measure on the nature of the design brief for the scheme and the relationship of the 'client' within the total process, there is a need to look carefully at the process whereby these projects are brought to fruition.

Under the old authorities there were in many instances complete departmental independence fortified by a committee structure whose members jealously guarded their domains against the assault from within, i.e., from other departments. In recent years there have been moves to look more closely at the interdependence of various stages within the totality of the construction process from conception to completion. The effect of departmental independence was fully exposed during the days of large scale slum clearance. The time scale for the initiation of the first intention to declare a slum clearance area to the date when all was redeveloped and occupied spread over ten years or more in some cases. There was no sense of corporate identity and responsibility. For example, land would lie derelict for years before the next stage was designed instead of co-ordinating the whole process. These processes involve legal procedures, compulsory purchase orders, appeals, physical planning of the concept with the contribution from highways, the statutory undertakings, the other aspects of the infrastructure, schools, play areas, etc., besides the important task of designing the dwellings themselves.

There was not only the necessity to co-ordinate various departments and activities, but if the professional independence was not to run riot, there had to be control and, if need be, directives given. It should be appreciated that professionals, and in particular those associated with design are highly individualistic, guarding their domains, and in some instances believing they have a divine right to revise their designs even during construction and regardless of the financial consequences for their clients. They do not react favourably to the discipline of management. One of the early tasks of the National Building Agency was to assist authorities in their management task, although those who were responsible for giving this

advice were themselves professionals and not managers by inclination and training.
Hence the early steps were to appoint co-ordinators with Town Clerks' departments,
but without executive functions. The next stage in the search for a solution was
the appointment of Directors of Development, or as some were styled, Directors of
Technical Services. Whatever the title, it was an attempt to bring under the
umbrella of a single individual the management responsibility for development. The
integration of all the necessary functions is still not complete to-day, for the
independence of the requisite legal services and the responsibility for controlling
the design of the highways often remains outside the job description for such a
Director.

The slow progress towards a corporate approach to the development process is to be
welcomed, but it still has a long way to go. Some of the tasks which local government has to undertake in determining its organisational structure is the identification of lines of activities, and the relationship with what I regard as the
service functions. This was discussed in the previous chapter. There is a need to
control the design load in respect of development schemes, just as it was stressed
that the workload for highway and transportation schemes needed to be monitored and
priorities established. All service functions must be within the control of the
line tasks if the priorities are to be achieved.

For those unfamiliar with the organisation of the construction activities, it
should be stated that for large commercial and industrial development, there is a
growing use of project managers who are charged with the management and the organisation of all activities concerned with the development. It may even include
economic appraisal of sites, schemes, etc. The post is one of management and
control and not positive involvement in the component activities. The danger of
using a professional who has executive tasks to perform in respect of that development is that his professional judgement will take precedence over managerial activities. It was interesting to note that many years ago the United Kingdom Atomic
Energy Authority adopted the principle that if the major design activity was
architectural, the Chief Engineer acted as project manager, and in those cases
where the engineering design was paramount, the Architect acted as the Project
Manager.

While most directors have long removed themselves from the drawing board, their
emotional involvement remains within their specialisms. Unless there is a strong
evidence of managerial ability, the appointment of Director of Development may as
far as project control is concerned be cosmetic, in that the emotional ties with
their own discipline may be stronger than the devotion to managerial duties and
tasks. This is another instance of the need for managerial training in all departments. Whatever structure is established for project planning control the importance of the task cannot be over-emphasised, and until the nature of this work is
appreciated it is unlikely that the structure will enable the tasks to be effectively managed and controlled.

Need Project Development be all 'In House'?

When local authorities deal with development for council houses and for other
municipal purposes, they often have considerable expertise and skills available
within them to undertake the necessary work. Recently a number of councils have
been building houses for sale, however. The variety of procedures is endless, but
many authorities, for a mixture of reasons, adopt an attitude of suspicion towards
private development in consequence of which they start to take on tasks for which
they have little or no expertise. The reason advanced for this suspicion is the
recurrence or fear of jerry building or inadequate supervision, but it can amount
to downright hostility towards developers as such. It is, however, a fact that
the average length of time to build municipal houses is substantially longer than

that for private developers. The reasons for this are not within the scope of this book, but it arises in some measure from local authority involvement. When the authorities design and seek tenders, contractors have no managerial responsibility for dovetailing the design process into the production programme. The contract itself allows for the payment of claims for delays caused by designers, so that the sense of urgency which a contractor has when undertaking speculative development for himself, is largely removed when under contract to a local authority.

If the same system of contracting exists when the authority builds houses for sale, the pressures to complete quickly are no different than if the houses when built are municipally owned. If on the other hand, all or nearly all of the responsibility for the scheme rests financially and operationally with private enterprise, then commercial forces come into play. Resistance to the use of the developers' skills is due in some measure to the attitude of the staff within the local authority, who have been known to exert industrial muscle. A run-down of the municipal housing programme could leave spare design capacity, for example, within an authority which some believe could be used to design houses for sale. Unfortunately the interchangeability of design staff of a local authority with that of private offices is very limited indeed. Local authority housing on a grand scale has its own stereotype within an authority's area, unless council staff design teams are supplemented by the employment of outside architects. Many municipal architects are not conversant with the economies which the private sector architects often have at their fingertips. I well remember the case of another authority's architects doing some design work for the County Council. I have never witnessed such a lavish design, so lavish that even my political opponents gibbed at the prospect of permitting the ratepayers to pay!

There was an instance of the use of industrial muscle for increasing staff within the county engineer's staff of the Greater Manchester Council. The Department of Transport offered the county quick release of monies for the M62 extension from Eccles to Salford. There was no way that the design work could have been carried out within the required time scale by the existing staff. The minister therefore requested the appointment of outside consultants. Until the dispute was settled, the aim of the trade union was to have more design staff employed by the county engineer. A trade union based upon a particular employer, as in the case of the National Association of Local Government Officers (N.A.L.G.O.) tends not to look at the broader spectrum of the employment of professional skills. The fact that engineers are doing jobs must be gratifying to members of the profession, but for sectional interests to demand that design work is carried out within the local authority, rather than in private enterprise firms, can be construed as a powerful demonstration, even by professional engineers, of the use of industrial action as the means of furthering the political aims of municipalisation!

The logical outcome of acceding to such a request would be to have spare design capacity once this special scheme was satisfactorily designed, with the inevitable result that to keep this spare capacity occupied, they would have to design still more abortive schemes. It may be that the large number of schemes inherited by the G.M.C. was due to the excessive capacity at one time or another!

The first thing that councillors and senior officers must recognise is the limited experience of their staff compared with the totality of construction operations. One shudders to think what would have happened if the Forth, Severn and Humber bridges were designed, for example, by local authorities. To assume that because a person is an architect or an engineer he is capable of designing anything which comes within his discipline is to have a very naive view of differing skills needed both to design and control construction activities; but it is a view which appears to come all too easily to many inexperienced councillors.

Accepting the fact that at least as far as design is concerned, there are differing
approaches and skills, so it is in other aspects of private development. Nowhere
is this more pertinent than in marketing skills. The local authorities have no
marketing skills as such, officers often confusing marketing with selling. The
marketing of cultural activities requires a different approach to that which comes
naturally to local government officers and illustrates the point effectively.

When the G.M.C. was formed, it appointed an Arts Marketing Officer in conjunction
with the Arts Council of Great Britain. It was clear to those councillors (they
were very few indeed) who took the trouble to know and understand the problem of
marketing the arts, that the traditional structure and procedure of an authority
(including financial control) was alien to the commercial approach needed. There
was considerable scepticism amongst certain officers when the concept of a combined
travel and theatre ticket for council sponsored productions was suggested. The co-
operation of the transport executive, as a quasi-commercial governmental organisation, was not given wholeheartedly, and even British Rail had to be cajoled into
selling the combined tickets. Once they realised that they might get additional
passengers the penny seemed to drop and they entered into the venture with enthusiasm.

On other occasions, discounts and special offers were advocated. When a successful
venture was completed, the internal auditors descended like flies because they
could not understand that there could be financial propriety. There was a distinct
atmosphere of distrust of such commercialism amongst many senior officers and
councillors, who felt that marketing, necessary as it was to the successful promotion of cultural activity, was in some way tainted. The success of the schemes was
only grudgingly accepted.

There are other aspects of the local authority's involvement in building houses for
sale. There are two extremes. At the one end the council grants a developer a
licence to build houses (i.e., the developer pays a fee for the right to build
houses on the land, the ownership of which remains with the authority until the
conveyance to the new owner is complete), and to undertake all the development work
as if it was the developer's own land; and at the other, for the council to let a
contract to a builder to construct such houses in the same way contractors build
municipal houses. In the latter case, the council will undertake two tasks in
particular which a developer would undertake. Often the best known developers act
as mortgage brokers to the potential buyers, giving advice on a range of methods to
finance the purchase, but this expertise is not part of the local authority's
function, especially when it offers 100% mortgages to potential purchasers as an
inducement. The second task is that of marketing, and I have already commented on
the fact that this skill is not part of the training needed for local government
duties. When it comes to a local authority acting as a building society, the
interest rates are less flexible than those available from building societies,
although it is possible that at the time of purchase there may be a shortage of
normal building society funds compared with local authority loans. It is clear that
with the widely fluctuating interest rates of the late 70's, it will not be long
before the average interest rate from building societies is about 1% lower than the
rate from local authorities. The methods by which the two sources of finance
operate are different, and it indicates once again that there are certain activities
for which local government involvement is less appropriate than those obtainable
from private enterprise.

My experience of local authorities undertaking the development process for building
for owner occupation is not encouraging. The authorities are not geared with the
requisite skills, and often they adopt the very worst attributes of private developers, in particular they fail to appreciate consumer problems and reactions. The
notion that because local authorities are in continuous operation and are unable to

go bankrupt like private developers, and are therefore able to look after the buyers on such matters as remedial work, is seldom borne out in practice. Some purchasers experience substantial delays which cause considerable aggravation.

The above demonstrates that there are numerous skills available in the private sector which many local authorities are reluctant to use, or decide not to use, possibly for the sake of civic pride. It should not be forgotten that the association with the development process is the nearest many councillors ever get to being entrepreneurs themselves. An acute observer can sometimes detect in councillors and officers a yearning to be successful business men, and undertaking the developments whereby the council builds for sale provides such an opportunity, and therefore it can be a temptation which some are unable to resist. Only those who are able to appreciate the role and function of a local authority, and the constraints placed upon it which are not present in the private sector, will understand that it is important for each sector to be free to use its expertise and so contribute its maximum effort to meet the various housing needs.

Before leaving the topic of building houses for sale, I would add that the role of central government can have an important impact upon the success or otherwise of a scheme, especially when the council decides to grant a developer a licence to build. There are two basic choices available to a council. Either it puts the licence out to tender, or fixes the licence fee and invites alternative schemes in terms of plans and costs, etc. If it is the former, there is a possibility that when the council adjudicates on alternative schemes from developers, that the Department of the Environment will veto any other consideration as being invalid, and will insist on acceptance of the lowest tender. If the latter course is adopted, the Department still has to approve the fee. So much for the freedom of local authorities to manage their affairs free of Whitehall and its regional satellites!

The use of Housing Associations

The Labour Party is 'hell bent' on municipalisation and is often unable to assess the merits and demerits of local authority involvement in projects. This is particularly true in respect of the use of voluntary agencies such as housing associations, which are considered suspect. Many labour party councillors condemn the voluntary housing movement out of hand and endeavour to use every piece of adverse publicity to support their attitude. National publicity in mid-1978 did not help the cause of the voluntary housing movement, but the political opposition indicates how political dogma can overrule objective assessments.

While it would be inappropriate to discuss in detail the contribution which the voluntary housing movement can make, it must be remembered that there is a tri-partite involvement of local authority, the Housing Corporation and the Department of the Environment.

At the time of writing, there is no doubt that this tri-partite involvement does not help councils complete the housing programme speedily. The dead hand of bureaucracy is very clearly illustrated as many schemes take an interminable time to come to fruition. The time-scales of meetings of the constituent parties seldom dovetail, and the local authority in particular, if it has a long cycle of meetings such as two months, does not help when the council, even for valid reasons, defers a decision which necessitates re-processing through the various committees. I have referred previously to the fact that it appears that government often dips its fingers into the 'till of time'. The tri-partite arrangement for housing associations is a classic example of how time is squandered by government and its agencies. It makes the problem of managing and controlling projects that much more difficult.

CHAPTER 11

The Code of Conduct for Those in Public Service or "Drink to Me Only"

The Royal Commission on Standards of Conduct in Public Life (1974-1976) under the chairmanship of Lord Salmon is the latest and most comprehensive report dealing with this subject. It is therefore appropriate for some discussion to take place on the state of affairs as seen by a councillor some three years after the report's presentation to Parliament.

The importance of both central and local government, nationalised industries and other public bodies in their client role as the initiator of contracts, cannot be underestimated, particularly when the money involved accounts for an ever increasing proportion of our Gross National Product. Where local authorities grant planning permission, various licences to trade and the provision of certain facilities consequent upon the increased legislation regulating both public and private activities, there are often considerable financial implications at risk if consents are not obtained. However, there is a great danger that the nation is demanding two standards of conduct; one for its public servants, and another for the private sector. Judging by the press reports, the private sector seems to be involved in activities which the Royal Commission in its recommendations sought to prevent from becoming commonplace in the public sector. It was natural that the Royal Commission report contained references to inability due to its terms of reference to report on the standards of conduct in the private sector. The public appears to accept this duality of standards.

It is a sad reflection upon society in general if it is willing to accept the spirit of the law designed to prevent corruption and bribery in public life, yet seems unperturbed when a former leading figure in public life, after serving his sentence for corrupt practices, has stated on television that the "ends justified the means". When there appear to be substantial benefits to the community arising from various schemes initiated by public bodies, there is a reluctance to ask too many questions about the procedure used to achieve the end result. Whenever you visit the North East, for example, it is impossible not to recognise the benefits which have accrued in that area from the initiatives of Mr. T. Dan Smith. Such a recognition is not to grant any seal of approval to his methods, but it is tragic when outstanding leadership leads people to use unethical means in order to achieve their objectives. Yet others are often involved and bear an equal responsibility. It will be even worse if the only method to overcome the dead hand of bureaucracy is that in order to achieve very desirable goals, it is necessary to resort to forms of corruption. However, once this attitude of the ends justifying the means becomes accepted by the general public, the law becomes inadequate to deal with the problem, due to fewer people being prepared to give evidence.

Whether we have yet reached this state of affairs is open to question, but it is clear that we are fast approaching the time when standards which we associate with certain overseas countries may become more common in this country at least in the private sector. Such a situation will have its own repercussions within the public sector before long.

It must be remembered that overseas corruption is a way of life and is not regarded as being reprehensible. Some twenty years ago, a colleague of mine visited West Africa and he estimated that the current rate of 'dash', as it is known, was around $12\frac{1}{2}$%; some four years ago on a similar visit we estimated that it had reached the order of 25%. The effective tender price when submitting a tender for a contract was to all intents and purposes inflated by the amount of 'dash' to be paid! In addition the situation had arisen that the first payment under the con- tract, sometimes made before work commenced, was related to the amount of commiss- ion due! I should add that an attempt was made at the commencement of General Gowon's term of office as the Federal Head of State of Nigeria, to root out corrup- tion, but most of the State Governors were so lax in following through the progr- amme of reform that it collapsed through lack of effectiveness. Recent publicity would seem to indicate that british companies are following similar practices over- seas on the basis, 'when in Rome, do as the Romans do'. British companies, there- fore, are almost forced into a position of adopting one practice within the U.K. and another for working in certain overseas countries. Will such practices be amongst the invisible imports? If people doubt the possibility of this, then I would inform them that as recently as November 1978, when visiting an exhibition at Birmingham, two members of a company talked to me openly about the "measures to express appreciation" that were avilable in respect of local council contracts. Incidentally I passed these comments on to the appropriate quarter - to use the standard terminology.

A cynic might be inclined to the view that in other countries the attitude is more honest in that the bribe takes place prior to the provision of a service, whilst in the U.K. it is often given after performance as a 'thank you'; or to put it another way, they show their appreciation in the usual way! I believe that such talk would have been unthinkable ten years ago. However I would not like to think that this attitude was general, as I know a number of companies which are scrupul- ously honest. It is a sign of the times that court cases are more frequent than hitherto. If we do not want matters to deteriorate, a code of contract has to be enforced very strictly. It is therefore pertinent to comment on the Parliamentary position.

My impression is that Parliament is less open about some matters than is the case in certain local authorities. The parliamentary register of interests remains voluntary, due to the attitude of one member in particular; yet a number of local councils have by resolution required the completion by its elected members of such a Register of Interests. These registers are sometimes open to scrutiny by members of the public. It is clear that such registers, both at Westminster and for any public body, provide a means to check whether a pecuniary interest has arisen and if annual updating of the register is undertaken there is a useful reminder of the need for elected members to be on the alert against the possibility of infringing a code of conduct.

However, no such open register exists in respect of paid servants, although the obligation to declare pecuniary interests is the same as for the elected members. Memory can play tricks, and without such an open register with its constant up- dating, the position remains unsatisfactory. The abuse of pecuniary interest is fairly easy to detect, but the receipt of gifts in kind or by service is more difficult to establish. These are the more serious forms of corruption to which local councillors and members of other public bodies, as well as officers, are constantly exposed.

Both Mrs. Ward-Jackson and Lord Houghton in their addendum to the Royal Commission went further than the Commission by referring to the root causes of the lowering of standards and the means to maintain them. Mrs. Ward-Jackson listed nine points worthy of attention. They reflected the problem which still exists over two years later.

The first refers to the attendance allowance which has replaced the former 'loss of earnings' payments. She stresses that the level of attendance money is such that it cannot compensate for loss of earnings, especially in respect of the chairman of committees who might spend as much as 40 hours a week on official business, often sacrificing overtime, promotion or other benefits of employment. Yet both she and Lord Houghton state that persons in receipt of these sums are sniped at by the media as if they were lining their pockets! Such attacks, they contended, do not help to secure the best possible candidates who are prepared to offer themselves for election. In addition, it increases the possible alienation of the elected member from the electorate. This public reaction to payments for those engaged in public service of this nature is a possible legacy from the role the councillors played in the large number of smaller authorities prior to reorganisation, when both the time involved and the responsibilities borne were less. Some conscientious councillors spend up to 70 hours a week - week-ends are seldom free from duties or counselling - that a maximum reimbursement for five days of committee meetings of £50 (prior to January 1979) seems derisory, when many councillors have stationery, postage and sometimes telephone calls and consequential bills to meet out of the attendance allowance.

Both Mrs. Ward-Jackson and Lord Houghton referred not only to the pressure for the less conscientious member to be a target for corruption in consequence of this situation, but to the fact that many councillors are paid less in their employment than many officers with whom they have to deal.

The relationship between officers and leading members of the council is another potential problem area especially where undue pressure is brought by one upon another. Most long-serving councillors have seen the dangers of this. Reports appear from time to time in the grass roots type of publication on such relationships, a point which did not escape Mrs. Ward-Jackson when she affirmed that many of the recent corruption cases arose out of the investigatory forms of journalism, such as "Private Eye", or the media, and not from any official source such as the Ombudsman, the District Auditor or internal disclosure. This dependence on a form of private detection rather than revelation from within public bodies is extremely disturbing if the nation is serious in its intent to stamp out corruption.

The district audit has not been a very successful vehicle for detecting corrupt practices. It was unable to uncover the Poulson affair although it came near to it. The process of auditing itself is unlikely to uncover the payment or receipt of bribes. The role of the audit vis-a-vis the police is somewhat obscure, although the latter would, I am sure, emphatically deny it. The police, in my own experience of reporting what I consider to be malpractices, require a signed statement from an eye-witness before they start any extensive investigation. The District Auditor is under no obligation to report back to a complainant, but only to the council on the accuracy or otherwise of the accounts. If therefore an individual suspects malpractice or has information given to him which leads him to have suspicions, the use of the official machinery is of little use. He must carry out studies of his own and lay the evidence himself as an eye-witness of events to support the contention before any satisfactory investigation can get under way. Unless you have the support of newspapers or the media this can be costly, not to mention time-consuming. In such a situation, little wonder that there is a tendency to brush aside suspicions and let sleeping dogs lie!

Revelations of corruptions occur almost by accident and more recently through bankruptcy proceedings - another matter which doesn't escape Mrs. Ward-Jackson. If Poulson had not been made bankrupt would anybody have dared to come forward and give evidence of corruption? If discovery is, as it were, a result of an accident of business, how much more is unrevealed? Is it the tip of the iceberg? I am reluctant to come to this conclusion, yet I am forced by my conversations with a number of officers to suspect that it is far more widespread than many are prepared to believe, let alone accept.

There is a facet of disclosure through bankruptcy which needs serious attention. In the many recent cases involving construction activity the resultant work was often of an acceptable standard; why then is it necessary to resort to corruption in order to remain in business? Is it not possible for honest people to get work from a public authority? I believe that it is, but in certain parts of the country where power has resided in too few hands for too long, the temptations appear to be too strong for some individuals.

This highlights the danger of prolonged political domination of a council. If the political complexion changes at fairly frequent intervals the chances of uncovering corruption are increased. What goes for the political complexion of councils goes for the office-holders too! Some political parties limit the period during which a person may hold the chairmanship of a committee. This limitation of tenure helps to provide a possible precaution against undesirable practices.

There is always a danger that liberty will breed licence unless controlled. Similarly the positions of power will in time corrupt or tend to corrupt the best of human beings, and therefore limited tenure remains the best safeguard against such malpractices among the elected members. Unfortunately such a turnover of chairmanships and political power is not universal. Where this is not possible, the electors and the parties involved have only themselves to blame if corruption is subsequently uncovered. However, the recent spate of trials may well be a salutary deterrent.

Even where political power does change from time to time, it is not unknown for some majority parties to hold all seats on the vital policy committee. Such a situation can be equally dangerous and conducive to suspicion of malpractices. It has often been suggested that open government will limit hidden deals, which may or may not have a corrupt element. The Local Government Act 1972 laid down the principle that committee meetings shall be open to the public, and that the exclusion of the public on the grounds that open discussion would be prejudicial to the public interest has to be moved as a resolution and passed before exclusion of the public is operative. However, public access to discussions does not extend to meetings of sub-committees. It is not unknown for councils to make extensive use of sub-committees, e.g. planning sub-committees, which may have delegated powers from the council, in which case decisions affecting residents are still made behind closed doors.

Another aspect of the openness of government is the apparent naive belief by the government that if the minutes of meetings are, as of right, available to the public all will be well. Many councils provide very brief minutes. What for instance does "that the report be accepted" really mean to the outsider without the opportunity for a sight of the report itself?

Like the restriction of the admission of the public to committees, and especially

sub-committees, the right to the sight of the minutes is equally inadequate. The
right of the public to full access to reports, except where it is clearly not in
the public interest, would do much to prevent corruption by allowing those with suspicions to make their own investigation and to satisfy themselves on the issues.
The only other way is for an investigator to open up his own channel for receiving
information through the leaking of official documents. At present, it is the disclosure by such leaks which provides the genesis of most investigations. Whether
this is the most desirable method, the reader must judge for himself. Without a
more open style of government, leaks will be the order of the day, and where they
occur, there will be a suspicion of deals, whether justified or not. While much
has been done in recent years to increase the exposure of local governments to
public scrutiny, it is extremely doubtful whether it is open enough even now. All
in public life must search their consciences to see if they are not unwittingly
contributing to suspicions.

It is inevitable that the media should concentrate on the instances of bribery
where they result from court cases; but these events do not happen without small
beginnings. To assume that it is only councillors who are most exposed to outsiders attention is to ignore the part played by officials with their innumerable contacts with those seeking business. We have, as a nation, been proud of our civil
service, but as it has grown over the years it was inevitable that the chance of
some officers conducting themselves below the expected standards would increase.
This growth in the number employed applies equally to both national and local
government.

Often the incidents of bribery and corruption grows almost imperceptibly from very
modest beginnings. I remember years ago, the relationship of an officer of a works
department with a number of councillors which grew in such a manner that eventually
when things within the department started to go wrong, there were very few
councillors who were not caught up in a net even in a small way! Eventually the
council had to resort to employing a private firm of accountants to look into the
operation of the department! One lady councillor used to receive a weekly bouquet
of flowers until her husband put a stop to it! It is very easy for innocent offers
of help by the use of council resources to become in time a normal feature of life.
Bearing in mind that corruption requires two people, such instances are likely to
arise when officers have motives to secure their own position, due to their own
unexposed inadequacies. I am unaware of a repetition of this state of affairs
existing to-day, but the opportunities are there, and councillors have to be very
careful not to compromise their position and therefore unable to exercise their
independent judgements.

Offers of hospitality in particular can be a path for the unwary. The common
source is the conference scene which affects a limited number of councillors and
officers. Here discretion is essential. The only way in which safeguards can be
written-in is for a report to be made to the appropriate committee of the conference with a reference to the hospitality received and its extent. Seldom do
officers and councillors attending conferences make any worthwhile reports. Few
councils make it standard practice. There is a case for writing such a requirement into the councils Standing Orders. Officers have numerous opportunities to
enjoy hospitality in the course of their day-to-day activities. In such instances
the regularity as well as the frequency has to be observed, to judge whether it
goes beyond the bounds when a sense of debt as to its propriety is created. I have
seen such hospitality and relationships develop over the years when I served as an
area secretary of an employers' association. Whether such relationships did lead
to corruption is impossible to tell; clearly the numbers of instances and the
extent of the hospitality was such that there was some indication that one firm was
receiving priority over others when assistance was sought from council officers.
Such occasions arose when there were brick shortages and surplus council stocks

were made available. I was informed that there was proper payment. The observed
hospitality however was to my mind evidence of a close relationship which exceeded
the bounds of discretion.

Recently I have received reports of hospitality being enjoyed on a scale which once
again gives rise to suspicion. I referred earlier to the very few exposures from
within an authority. I have been disconcerted that very few, if any, follow-ups
have taken place when matters have been reported to the establishment. In one or
two isolated instances, aspects involving alleged substantial gifts have been
looked at by amateurs rather than by professionals.

It is possible that reports of malpractice provided by members of the staff to a
councillor may be made out of pique or frustration. But it is often through such
reports that some light is shed on possible occurences. When I have received them
I have always passed them on to authorities, but the investigations have never in
my judgement been seen to be as thorough as I would have liked. While some police
chiefs adopt crime prevention campaigns against specific areas of concern, such as
pornography, drinking and driving, etc., there doesn't seem to be a campaign arising out of reports of possible corruption in public life to the same extent. Maybe
the investigations of suspicions are seen as being long and tedious. It is always
easier to start from a known fixed datum point, such as a signed statement setting
out times, details etc. of the alleged offence.

A more serious attempt should be made by councils themselves to stamp out possible
sources of corruption. In many cases, the Conditions of Service are inadequate
in covering the receiving of gifts and hospitality. There is always the chance
that the innocent practice may become something bigger in time and, if there was a
clear established procedure covering such matters, it might be that the recent
corruption might have been prevented.

It is clear that the law makes the receipt of rewards a criminal offence, but what
constitutes a reward when it comes to hospitality and the receipt of small gifts,
is less precise . It must be expected that from time to time business discussions
should be continued over a meal; it is standard practice in both the private and
public sectors. There are in addition association and institutional dinners held
outside working hours which can lead to the cementing of business as opposed to
social relationships. I remember one County Planning Officer who was so scrupulous
about these matters that he never attended any association dinner, even as the
official guest of the association, in order not to be seen to be taking hospitality
from those who might at some stage require his services. Not all officers apply
such strict rules to their own conduct.

The border line between business lunches, etc., and overt hospitality, can be very
thin! On the question of gifts, the seasonal present can be another matter.
Clearly gifts like calendars which are part of legitimate advertising are accepted
as such. The private sector has exchanged the bottle(s) over the years, but such
a procedure involving a local authority officer is unacceptable. However, I have
received reports of such gifts being made, but when reported they have not been
investigated in the manner I would have expected!

It was because of the thin red line dividing the business lunch, etc. from habitual
hospitality that during my term as a councillor on the Greater Manchester Council
I protested at the lack of any precise code of conduct in respect of hospitality.
This protest was made consequent upon the publication of the Commission's report.
As a result, the following was incorporated in the Personnel Manual and Staff hand-
book: "Where any question of a gift or hospitality arises staff should immediately
consult either their chief officer or the appropriate assistant chief officer".
The important thing in my judgement concerning hospitality of any kind involving a

LOCAL GOVERNMENT

potential business relationship is that the senior officer of the department concerned should be informed. It then becomes the duty of that officer to check upon the frequency and admissibility of such invitations etc. in the light of circumstances. However, it is one thing to have such a code, it is another to check that it is being adhered to by all concerned. It is essential that adherence to such a code should be incorporated in the appropriate disciplinary codes of the authorities. This would do much to strengthen the position and help to keep the whole matter within bounds. Without such surveillance these will continue to be reports of wining and dining, which causes resentment amongst junior staff and has a disastrous effect upon staff morale. Let us hope that such a procedure will become standard throughout local government in the very near future.

CHAPTER 12

Area Committee or Delegation that Isn't

The first election to the new councils took place in 1973, but for a year before there had been working parties formed from the constituent authorities of the new districts to prepare the ground for reorganisation. Stockport was fortunate to have as a leading member of that working party and subsequently of the new authority, someone who was fully conversant with the operation of a district council, yet through his business interests had served as a member of the County Borough. It was this awareness of the advantages of smaller units that helped in a large measure to establish an area system throughout the new organisation.

It is important to understand the nature of this system. It is being monitored by the Local Government Unit of Birmingham University with financial assistance from the Department of the Environment. It is not appropriate to anticipate its report, except to say that it is likely to be an excellent exposition of the situation as it exists within Stockport and the other authorities being studied. Whether it will make any fundamental contribution to the future development of this concept of local authority structure, I have serious reservations at the time of writing, due to the limited contacts and discussions with its team.

The area organisation has two facets, the political set-up and the management structure of the council. Taking the political set-up first, it should be viewed as part of the process of linking the various area committees through to the standing committees of the council, so that a sense of involvement of the community in the discussions can be engendered. Each community so identified was destined to have a community council - not all parts of the borough were covered. These community councils were elected at a general meeting open to all electors within the designated community area. Initially these elections were advertised by a door-to-door distribution of the requisite convening notice. The Community Councils were designed to be non-political in that no party literature, canvassing or campaigning, as we have come to know it, took place. This, however, did not prevent the political parties viewing the composition with interest!

The community councils are able to enjoy a special relationship with the council through:-

a) the right to grant-in-aid for their activities from the authority

b) acceptance of a standard constitution drawn up by the authority

c) the right of the elected executive committee to meet the area committee twice a
   year to discuss matters of special and mutual interest.

d) to preclude councillors from election to membership of the community council,
   but with a right to attend its executive committee meetings as ex-officio
   members,

In one or two areas, community councils or similar bodies were of long standing,
had undertaken various activities which successfully engendered a community
spirit. They effectively undertook the part played by the old style Parish
Councils in places where none existed previously. However, for these councils to
come within the ambit of the Stockport structure and to receive benefit therefrom,
their constitutions had to conform to the council's standard format.

There is little doubt that the Community Councils do serve a useful purpose in permitting a number of people who are interested in their own community, but who do
not wish to serve as councillors (or who have been unsuccessful at its polls!) to
think deeply about problems with which the local community is faced. However, in
a number of cases, it seeks to think up ideas to do. More important, the greatest
drawback to their operation and influence is the fact that they tend to be mirrors
of the full council. I shall never forget the time when the community councils were
suddenly asked by the authority to consider the various policy options and rate expenditure items in respect of the forthcoming budget. This was an attempt by the
officers to encourage involvement, yet in every case there was no back-up of official data and information necessary to make an informed judgement. It seemed crazy
to ask the community councils to undertake this task which preoccupies the full
council some three months of discussions in various committees.

It would have been feasible for the community councils to be effective politically
if they had powers. They have degenerated in large measure into political impotency.
Even if representatives from the community councils could be treated as members of
the appropriate area committee and with power to vote, then they would start to
exert influence. It must be appreciated that the area committees have no executive
powers. They are a sounding board for matters of concern throughout the area
regardless of topic. This is not a far-fetched proposal since there are members of
governing bodies of schools who are not councillors. Such members have the right
to vote and to make a limited number of decisions within the remit of school managing bodies. As stated earlier, the area committees are not executive bodies, but
only advisory and, therefore, in no way will they be taking decisions away from the
elected members of the council if representatives from the community councils served
on them.

It is true that more people vote at the council elections than at the election for
membership of a community council, but this is due to the latter's election taking
place at a meeting where attendance qualifies the elector to vote. If the election
to the community council could take place at the same time as, and in conjunction
with the authority's own election, it would open the whole procedure to the elect-
ioneering process but would ensure that its membership had a broader base than at
present. The council decided against permitting this course of action. If it had
been accepted, then the resultant council would have been more akin to the Parish
Council which still exists in certain areas. Unfortunately this was not a solution
which the local authority could determine. The basis for making an application to
the Secretary of State to establish a Parish Council did not accord with the
Stockport scheme, since the newly-formed statutory Parish councils are based upon
the geographical area of the former District Council. Within Stockport the number
of areas considered to be communities as such, and therefore appropriate for the
establishment as a community council, would have required two or three such Parish
Councils within the former district boundaries. If legislation would permit the

establishment of Parish Councils in the place of the present Community Councils,
they would have statutory powers and be integrated far more effectively within the
local government structure. It might also provide a suitable stimulus for the
creation of such Parish Councils in a number of districts within large urban areas
such as the City of Manchester, where there is no such body able to act on behalf
of the local community.

There will be some who might argue that attendance of community council members at
meetings of the area committee will duplicate the work of the elected members to
the Borough Council. This is not strictly true, because the elected members have
the duty not only to represent their own ward, but also to make decisions which
affect the whole borough in just the same way that the locally-elected county
councillors have to have regard to county-wide considerations. Each council has a
clear function which it can perform. By and large it is the local community level
of organisation which is missing and its absence tends to entrench the frustration
felt by many people as a result of greater centralisation created by the reorganisation of local government.

It is the experience of most community councils, especially those established with
a flourish of activity arising out of a local issue, that there is difficulty in
finding people to stand as candidates for election to them. Some councils have not
the requisite number of elected members, which indicates that the concept could
have been wrong, or that their apparent impotency could be due to the fact they
were given the wrong task in the first place.

Unless measures are taken through legislation to designate community councils as
statutory Parish Councils with limited powers, the initial establishment of community councils may well prove to have been fruitless, yet it is invaluable to have an
established body capable of becoming the focus of corporate opinion and action
within a community. There is an undoubted need for a group to look carefully at
those facets of community life which are best carried out by voluntary effort, than
by a local authority which tends to be more impersonal and regulated by bureaucratic
machinery.

For some time I have believed that the present community councils within Stockport
should have a much closer link with the various voluntary organisations operating
within the community areas. Some voluntary organisations cover a wide area, but
the establishment of some link even to assist in the task of co-ordination and, if
possible, of identifying those areas of need which are not catered for adequately,
would be invaluable. The stumbling block to any development in this direction as
far as Stockport is concerned lies in the constitution of the community councils,
laid down by the borough and controlled by it through the special relationship and
the receipt of grant-in-aid.

The community council should be able to include within its remit the functions of
a local Council for Social Service, providing a forum for inter-group help as well
as being an initiator of activities to meet local needs. To achieve this, the
constitution must permit the membership of the community councils to include representatives from various organisations within the community. If this arrangement
was operative it would be a powerful instrument to inject a real community spirit,
to counterbalance the disadvantages from local government reorganisation.

To change the role of the community councils within Stockport towards a community
action based council rather than a debating society, requires a re-definition of
the special relationship with the Borough Council, and powers to be given to the
community council to use such grant-in-aid for long-term community projects. Such
a change means the recognition by councillors and officials alike that local authorities do not have to be the sole agency for major community activities.

The obstacle to such a change lies mainly in the attitude of some politicians, regardless of party, for it is one of their serious defects that some have developed over the years such a feeling of mental superiority over their fellows that they believe that they alone should hold the key to the destiny of their constituents. They seem reluctant to provide sufficient freedom of thought and action to such constituent organisations as community councils, or to believe that such councils will act responsibly in using grants. Instead they circumscribe the duties of such councils with excessive control and the threat of sanctions. Nowhere is this more in evidence than in the field of social service where the move towards bureaucratic direction and control of activities by central organisations is constantly increasing. This is an undesirable trend. Councils should relinquish wherever possible direct control in favour of giving financial assistance to those voluntary bodies which can provide a much more personal service. Throughout government there is a strong gravitational pull towards the centre which needs to be counterbalanced. In this the community councils have a valuable role to play.

If community councils are to be effective, however, they must be given more executive functions than hitherto, if there is to be any incentive for people to serve on them with the knowledge that they can achieve something worthwhile. There is a danger of these councils degenerating into talking shops. It needs to be stated that there are a number of able and public-spirited people who are endeavouring to make the present community councils work. How long their patience will last is another matter. The decline in the number of candidates willing to serve shows that those who remain on them have a loyalty and sense of public service worthy of emulation.

It is worth taking note of these areas where the former District Councils, based on small communities, have retained a very clear identity and spirit through the establishment of Parish Councils in their place. Determined people have refused to allow their identity as a community to decay or to succumb to the worst effects of reorganisation.

Turning to the area committee system as it operates in Stockport, reference has been made to possible membership of the area committees comprising the elected district and county counsillors with representatives of the appropriate community council. It is important to understand the role of these area committees, which are undoubtedly one of the success stories of Stockport. Other councils should seriously consider establishing them.

Area committees have no executive powers to make decisions as such, but members can request the officers to place on the agenda any item which affects any part of their area. Since these committees can cover two or three wards, the opportunity is available for six to nine councillors, plus one or more county councillors, to become more fully conversant with all the issues within the area. Unlike the old district councils where each ward was represented on the service committees of the district, a similar distribution of representation is not possible in the new councils otherwise the number of members serving on these service committees would be unwieldy. The area committees having items affecting a particular department on the agenda can call for a report from the officers concerned, which then becomes public knowledge because these committees are open to press and public. The officer's report and the subsequent discussion by various members of the area committee enables a member of the area committee to make a more effective contribution to the discussion at meetings of the service committee. The area committee system is held in respect by the chairman and members of the council's service committees. Very serious consideration is given to representations from the area committees since the latter comprises all parties serving the constituent wards. The rejection by a service committee of a unanimous recommendation by an area committee can cause embarrassment, if the party whip's direction runs counter to

the views stated at the area meeting. When area committee recommendations are
upset there can be heated debates, but due to the possibility of a reference to the
ombudsman, the major service committees are rightly cautious of ignoring local
opinion. Further, in case of any doubt as to the views of an area committee on a
particular topic, there is also a reference back to the area committee before a
final decision is reached. This may cause delays but it does ensure real consultation.

A number of developers do not necessarily like this arrangement whereby planning
applications can be re-processed through the area committee system. The delays in
making the final decision arises not from the system itself but is due to the
length of the cycle of meetings. While the area committee meets in the week prior
to the meeting of the planning committee and so ensures the minimum lapse of time
between the two meetings, the cycle is a four week one. Should a deferment be considered appropriate, then a further four weeks interval elapses. Unfortunately for
the developers there may be a substantial interval between the submission of an
initial application and its consideration by the area committee due to discussions
taking place between the planning officers and the developer to iron out any queries
before being placed on the agenda with the officer's recommendation. This procedure
is essential in order not to clutter the committee with unresolved planning queries.
The only way that these possible delays can be curtailed is by shortening the cycle
of meetings insofar as they affect planning applications. This is possible if the
cycle of planning meetings is of a different duration to that of the full council.
Stockport operates an eight week cycle with a four week cycle for the Planning
Committee which has full delegated powers. It would not be impossible to have a
three week cycle for planning purposes, since their decisions do not require
endorsement by the full council. It is likely that, should the full council cyle
be reduced to six weeks, a three week planning will be seen to be administratively
tidym and so overcome the concern faced by applicants for planning permission. It
would, however, be a disaster for the function of effective consultation on planning
matters if pressure from the State was put on councils to shorten still further the
time of deliberation on planning applications. It is a paradox of present thinking
which requires speedy determination on the one hand, and full consultation on the
other.

There are a few additional points worth making about the operation of the present
system and that proposed. There will be the argument that an area committee which
has representatives of the community council serving on it will reproduce the
anomaly which exists at meetings of school managers and governors, when the councillors alone receive an attendance allowance. This could be used as an argument
against the proposal, but it should however make central government reconsider the
method of compensating councillors for service. It may be appropriate at this
juncture to mention that councillors incur expenses on stationery, postage, travel
and telephone which are not always recoverable from the council. In many cases
these exceed the total amount received by way of attendance allowances. If a
councillor was given a fixed sum - different for the chairman and vice-chairman of
committees - then these anomalies would not exist, and could not then be used as an
argument for preventing reform of the membership of the area committees on the lines
suggested.

One feature of the area committee system which is often overlooked is that it is
not unknown for more members of the public to attend these meetings than attend
the main service committees. Large attendances are usual when there is a contentious planning application coming forward for discussion, but many of the public do
stay to hear discussions on other matters, especially when they have submitted a
complaint or a suggestion to a councillor for consideration. The area meeting is
held within the appropriate area and accordingly the public have less distance to
travel to attend than often is the case with meetings at the town hall. These

meetings also provide a useful contact between ratepayers and the councils' operations, especially when one or more officers have to present reports on various matters
and be questioned on it.

The reader should have some idea of the support which I consider the Area Committee
system deserves, as well as the functions which community councils should fulfil.
It is, however, another side of the area committee coin, namely the organisation,
which needs to be looked at more closely. In Chapter 9 and elsewhere the managerial structure and the way in which management operates has been fully discussed.
The area committee system has a possible counterpart in an area management structure.
In the possible approach to the topic of an area management we find the beiggest
clash of all between the centralists and the decentralists taking place, with the
latter invariably losing out. This state of affairs is due to a number of factors.

Firstly, there is the notion that control requires the immediate presence of the
controller, and that it is difficult, if not impossible, to control that which you
cannot see. Secondly, there is the fear arising from a possible co-ordinating role
being exercised at area level whereby juniors will tend to put their own interpretation on council policy and be free from possible restraints. The third factor,
and the one which provides the key, is the fear of delegation in the light of the
first factor, coupled with the departmental head's possible uncertainty as to the
capacities and capabilities of those responsible for the appropriate functions at
area level.

The constant exposure of local government to public criticism makes officers
naturally sensitive to criticism. Any lapse in performance concentrates the glare
of publicity on the offender. It would be natural therefore for seniors to
provide a screen to protect their staff from the predators of publicity. This
could result in a reluctance to delegate authority and responsibility. An area
management system requires a considerable amount of delegation to be effective, and
in consequence many senior officers are reluctant to support such a structure.
There are no fundamental organisational problems in establishing an area management
system other than that of establishing a framework within which council policy
decisions can be implemented, permitting the use of professional discretion backed-
up by an effective reporting system. Private industry has often done this as part
of its managerial development programme, but local authorities have talked about
management development as if it was a technique and not as a philosophy of management.

The case for an area management structure is enhanced by the corporate nature of
local authority activities at the point where the needs of the community are identified. For example, where there is a need for psychological advice for children
of school age, it may be necessary for the families involved to receive advice
based upon social service expertise. Such instances require the involvement of two
departments and because they are often due to a multiplicity of factors, this
situation is best dealt with by a team working closely together. Centralised
control of the departments concerned may not be able to provide local knowledge and
effective teamwork. The reason for centralising of the functions has little to do
with the effectiveness of teamwork, but more to adminstrative convenience and the
ease of immediate supervision, which can amount to direction which destroys the
concept of professional responsibility by those in junior posts.

The other major obstacle to the adaption of area management systems put forward by
its opponents is that of financial control. There is a reluctance amounting to
outright hostility by some Directors of Finance to giving others responsibility for
finance. A typical example of this was the old Cheshire county practice of providing head teachers with an imprest account, whereby they could call for work to be
carried out on their schools of an urgent nature by local contractors. Following

reorganisation, a complex system of works orders was substituted. These orders
have to be processed through a number of channels before work can commence by the
Direct Works Department, regardless of the time and effort needed by head teachers
on occasions to chase outstanding orders. No one appears to have done a costing
exercise to ascertain the real costs to the authority, including all the hidden
costs of time and effort chasing matters, let alone the possible additional staff
needed to cope.

It is difficult not to draw the conclusion that lurking behind all the moves towards centralisation is a basic fear by seniors of those whom they cannot see and
control. Those who pursue, even blindly, such a course are slowly strangling
initiative and development of their staff. Little wonder that the consequence is
that when councillors interview staff for some of the senior posts carrying very
substantial salaries, the quality of applicant is often unable to match expectations,
let alone be commensurate with salary!

Much therefore may be written by the Institute of Local Government Studies as a
result of its surveys on the topic of area organisation within the various authorities, but in the final analysis I maintain that the real dilemma facing local
government in any possible implementation of area management schemes is human
attitudes by those who wield power at the head of departments. If they have faith
in their own judgement of the capacity of their staff, and are prepared to give
them discretion to use their professional judgement and even to enjoy some financial
responsibility, then and only then, can area management be effectively implemented.
But equally the elected councillors must expect mistakes from time to time. The
only foolproof method is to have no discretion at all, and that will breed a whole
generation of professional morons. Few people with professional qualifications
will be satisfied with such a role.

There is a need for a word of warning to those who are advocates of such an area
management system linked with its political counterpart of area committee. The
argument will be put forward that such a situation will tend to turn the Area
committee into a mini-council, with the area team as its paid service counter-parts.
There is no intention in my advocacy of the area management system to transfer
executive powers from the central service committees to the area committees. The
link, however, between any area team of officers and elected members could be of
assistance in the co-ordination process so essential if the departmental mentality
is to be destroyed. One further benefit of the area management system will be to
foster the corporate nature of local government at junior level. Experience at
this level will provide a sound training ground for the development of corporate
management, which as we have seen in earlier chapters is the cinderella of all
management processes in local government; but a cinderella who hasn't yet reached
the stage of going to the ball!

CHAPTER 13

Can the Ratepayer Effectively Challenge the System?

The ratepayer has two possible channels of enquiry if he feels aggrieved at the actions of a local authority. He can refer matters either to the district auditor or to the ombudsman.

In the course of four years I have been concerned with two references to the local government ombudsman. Both of them concerned activities concerned with the planning procedures which are by far the most common causes of complaint the ombudsman receives. The first involved a redevelopment scheme for a corner site within a residential area. The scheme was not effectively processed in accordance with the council's declared procedure for consultation. The effect of this reference has been that subsequently the council has been meticulous in following its procedure of providing for consultation with those likely to be affected by developments. This has occurred even when there is a considerable likelihood of delaying the time when the council is required to make its final decision.

This consultative process does call for patience and a meticulous attention to the procedures for consulting those likely to be affected whenever development is proposed. While developers and others are very concerned at inordinate delays, it is impossible to reconcile the need for a full consultation with immediate decision making. Unfortunately developers assume that, after long and exhaustive negotiations with planning officers, the eventual decision is a process of rubber stamping. However, it is only when a plan is formally submitted, subsequent to these initial negotiations that the consultative process can start.

The replies received as a result of the consultation process are considered by the planning committee. Usually the observations take the form of requests for amendments pointing out alleged undesirable features. In some cases there is outright opposition. It is, therefore, unwise of any developer to submit a plan without first consulting the planning officer, so that some of the obvious grounds for possible objection may be noted, and if necessary the plan modified in the light of the officer's experience. There is always a danger arising from premature applications that unnecessary local opposition can be generated and carried over to the final applications. The fact that governments have given every encouragement for consultation to take place means that it has become the policy of many councils, and consequently when lapses in procedure occur references to the ombudsman have helped to ensure that nothing untoward occurs, or is likely to recur.

There was one interesting feature of my first submission to the ombudsman which he

was unable to resolve because it involved a matter of law. It is a point which
parliament itself has not tackled but which does create problems when applications
for certain types of outline planning permission for development are submitted. In
this case there was an outline scheme for nine flats which in the accompanying plan
showed them to be accommodated within the curtilage of the existing dwelling.
There was considerable local opposition at the time of the application to any possible extension of development on this site. This view was shared by many local
councillors. When the details of the scheme were submitted for approval, however,
the area of the proposed building was substantially increased over that set out in
the original outline application and was, therefore, considered to be over-develop-
ment of the site. The planning officers maintained that the nine flats required a
larger site if they were to be of an acceptable spatial standard. The crucial
question which arose was, is the outline planning permission which contained a
clearly defined curtilage of the development operative in respect of the curtilage
shown on the outline application, or the number of units, namely nine flats?
Clearly in this instance, when outline application was approved, these two facets
of the development were incompatible.

It is my submission that the officers were at fault in recommending approval and
allowing the committee without an appropriate comment to approve the outline application where there were these two irreconcilable facets contained within it. The
officers appeared not to have done their sums, for it must be remembered that the
planning committee consists of lay people who cannot be expected to do the necessary
measurements on the plans to check whether there are aspects which are incompatible,
and therefore need to be resolved before the permission is granted. This is the
officers' task. Such a situation can, of course, be overcome by specifying in the
approval the conditions under which such a permission is granted, i.e. either
leaving the curtilage to be decided at detailed planning application stage, or
granting permission for a change of use with the number of units to be decided later.
It is of course preferable for the incompatibility to be pointed out to the potential developer as early as possible, so that these problems are not built-in with
the subsequent opposition becoming inflamed by what the local residents believe to
be inadequate checking by the Town Hall staff. Such situations give rise to the
possibility of complaints being submitted to the ombudsman.

The second submission to the ombudsman also involved a planning matter. The general
complaint of the residents concerned the manner in which the council controlled the
development. There were two main grievances. The first concerned the landscaping
scheme which appeared to be constantly delayed, to the detriment of neighbouring
properties, and could not by any stretch of the imagination be described as landscaping. It took an inordinate amount of time, following representations by the
local residents, for a satisfactory scheme to be carried out. The second grievance
arose out of the actual siting of a particular dwelling. As explained earlier, the
council had extensive consultative procedures which were followed in this case, but
one fact was never drawn during those consultations directly to the attention of
those consulted, and this could have accounted for much of the correspondence and
ill-feeling which increased as time elapsed. It was that the original plot numbers
1-7 were changed in the course of the development to the extent that plot no. 1 at
the original consultation stage became plot no. 7. The original numbered plots
2-7 were submitted in one application for approval of the details, but when the
original plot no. 1 was submitted, it had been re-numbered no. 7. Unfortunately
those more closely concerned with the development of the original plot no. 1 were
not notified of this re-numbering and assumed that when they were notified of the
application of the new no. 7 that it concerned the plot furthest away from them.
As a result there were no objections or observations recorded when the detailed
planning permission for this particular plot came before the committee for approval.

It was only when work started that the stark reality of the situation was revealed

to those who had they been aware of the re-numbering would have made submissions to
the council. These problems never seem to come singly, they appear to act as
magnets for other problems. This time it included the submission of inaccurate
drawing of the site plan and further, during the course of construction the developer deviated from his plan for the dwelling to a considerable extent, changing the
use of the garage and repositioning certain retaining walls. Many of the deviations
were corrected following the issue of enforcement notices by the council; but to
require, as the objectors sought, the re-siting of the building by moving it a few
feet to comply with the permission because the builder either could not read draw-
ings, or decided that the exact position was immaterial, was considered to be taking
the enforcement proceedings to a limit which the courts might not be willing to up-
hold.

The ombudsman decided after a preliminary investigation not to continue his
enquiries on this submission because he was satisfied that some of the procedures
operated by the council, of which the complainants had been critical, had been
remedied during the course of the correspondence leading up to the reference.
Among them was the failure to record dates and times of meetings with the builder
and developer together with the decisions arrived at, at these meetings. It also
involved the role of the building inspectorate and the planning officers who should
have had a very close liaison. The building inspector makes numerous visits to
ensure compliance with the building regulations, and if unnecessary duplication of
visits is to be avoided he should alert the planning officers to any deviation from
approved plans. While it could be held that the complaint was not upheld, it must
be recorded that the knowledge that an aggrieved party had the opportunity to make
such references, coupled with the correspondence of a persistent councillor on behalf of those aggrieved did make the officers review their procedures and practices.
While there may be little satisfaction in such instances for an aggrieved party,
the process which is initiated do es tend to change things for the future. Such
references do keep authorities on their toes. I have always held that you don't
have to record a formal submission to gain a victory!

Incidentally it is worth recording that it is not unknown for whole developments to
be turned round through ninety degrees and the building to be substantially complete
before the officers become aware that something is amiss! It behoves councillors
to ensure that those responsible for supervision of development cover all aspects
during the progress of the work and, at least, take a copy of the approved plans
along to check!

The second channel which a ratepayer may use to challenge a council's procedures
and actions is by challenging the accounts at the annual audit of the authority's
accounts. The difficulty which a ratepayer faces is knowing when that audit takes
place; for while it may be advertised in the local press in the usual way, few
people have a daily routine of scouring the papers in case there should be the
statutory notice advertising the audit. The statutory procedure of advertising the
audit is neat and tidy as far as the authority is concerned, but it can make it
difficult in practice for an individual ratepayer, since there is no obligation
even to inform councillors that the audit is due. I cannot recall an instance
whilst serving in the G.M.C. when the attention of councillors was drawn to the
submission of the accounts to the district auditor. The notice could have been
tucked away in the minutes or incorporated in the epitome of them under "other
routine matters"!

The right to challenge the accounts is vested in every ratepayer. Fortunately the
duties of the district auditor are not confined to conducting audits. There is a
continuing commitment in respect of any matter raised with him concerning on-going
matters, which are drawn to his attention outside the period when he is conducting
the official audit. The possible dilemma which an objector must face is the

position of privilege of the communication between the objector and the district
auditor. This protection of privilege is only available during the period of the
audit and on matters pertaining thereto. However, if the objector is sure of his
ground there is little reason for concern at the lack of privilege in the case of
a reference being made outside the audit period.

There will be many cases when a reference to the district auditor is the only
effective means whereby various activities of the council can be challenged and
come under the scrutiny of an independent person. This was the case when I first
raised a matter with the district auditor. This occurred in 1973 during the preparation for the reorganisation of local government, and therefore the formal hearing of the objection took place during the last days of an urban district council.
It turned out to be a particularly inauspicious time to make such a reference.
Many officers in the treasurer's department were applying for posts with the new
emerging authorities. It didn't help them for it to be known by rumour that the
district auditor was undertaking a major investigation into the accounts. District
auditors, I gather, often take the opportunity provided by such a reference, even
on a minor matter, to delve deeper than would otherwise be the case. To be fair to
the officers concerned I did write to the new shadow council that the reference
which I had initiated did not arise out of any malpractices within the treasurer's
department, but as a result of alleged inadequate supervision in the surveyor's
department; therefore the only way open to a ratepayer who could not obtain satisfaction through direct correspondence was to use the statutory right to challenge
the accounts.

The reference arose out of the concern of local residents of a particular road
where they contended that certain work executed in one year had been redone in conjunction with other work in the following year. There were suggestions that some
of the new kerbing stones and channels had been replaced in the subsequent year,
and that the work had been indifferently carried out. In response to these allegations the council sought outside opinion on the efficiency of the operation and
satisfied themselves on a number of matters. Time alone has testified to the
justification of the allegations, but it was difficult to determine the long-term
effect of the quality of the construction work at the time when the complaint was
lodged.

When it came to the formal hearing of the objections to the accounts by the
district auditor, it was discovered that the dimension books of the clerk of works
responsible were destroyed some ten days prior to the hearing, as they were having
a clear-out before handing over to the new authority! These documents being
primary records would have established the validity or otherwise of the resident's
allegations. The case, therefore, fell by default, and had to be withdrawn due to
this destruction of evidence.

The next instance of a submission to the district auditor is almost a continuing
saga and dealt with a number of items concerning the operation of a section of one
of an authority's departments. The reference included evidence of overtime being
paid but not worked, as well as a number of matters concerning the selection and
the use of plant.

Copies of time sheets were supplied. In addition there was personal observation
of sites which indicated that all was not well The district auditor considered
the whole matter, but he decided that while the practice of paying overtime without
any work being done might be considered undesirable, there was no abuse since there
was evidence that these payments fell within the category of protected earnings!
Earnings extant on 31st March 1974 are protected, and this protection extended to
the method of compilation. The protection arose out of the regulation promulgated
under the Local Government Act 1972. It should be borne in mind that the extent

of these excess overtime payments involved 10 hours or more a week!

Under the circumstances, the objection had no effect. What is very disturbing indeed in the light of the district auditor's decision is that the officers of the council, if they had done their homework, should have reported the situation to the personnel committee when the overtime situation was under review by that committee. At no time were the 'protected' overtime payments indicated in any report. Accordingly the councillors would be justified in assuming that there was no protection of earnings involved when the data relating to overtime was presented to them.

For a considerable period I consistently challenged the operation of the refuse disposal operations of the Greater Manchester Council. A considerable amount of information was provided by a number of employees who considered that malpractices were prevalent. The list was long. It concerned the overtime situation referred to earlier, and a number of items concerning mechanical plant, such as the apparent loss of the protective plates fixed under the vehicles to prevent damage to the engine and transmission from metal deposited in the refuse, the scrap value of replaced tracks for crawler vehicles, the alleged shortfall in income from those commercial concerns using the refuse tip. The main concern centred round the selection of plant for use on these tips. There was a decision early in the life of the Council to standardise the plant to be used. Such a decision had considerable advantages in such matters as obtaining spares, etc. However, the new authority had little data upon which to select its plant as the necessary historical records of alternative plant which might have been available in the archives of the former authorities were not handed over. The technical advice available within the authority was limited. The officers concerned who were formerly with one of the constituent authorities were without the benefit of experience of large scale operations unless outside advice was sought. No such advice appeared to have been sought in this instance.

The use of plant for working on refuse tips is a specialised task. It was, therefore, disconcerting to hear from one of the councillors who visited the public works exhibition that he and his colleagues approved the selection of a particular item of plant because it "appeared easy to drive". Not the soundest judgement upon which to select such plant! It is not only local authorities who operate tips, yet there appeared to be a total lack of consultation with private industry on the relative merits and demerits of the performance of various plant. The one fact that emerged from discussions over a long period of time was that not only was the wrong type of plant being used, but not even the right tyres! The latter contention seems to be borne out by the number of stoppages due to punctures, but above all the failure to use appropriate wheels to increase compactness and so prolong the life of the tips. This is even more remarkable when the short life left for the existing tips was the major concern of the authority!

With such a catalogue of what I can only describe as inadequate managerial control which affects every ratepayer within the local authority, it could be assumed that the district auditor might be able to ensure that changes ensued. Unfortunately, in spite of submissions to him, I came up against the problem of establishing the exact abuse or illegality, since this is the extent of his remit. It is perfectly legal for a council to select inadequate plant, be stupid in the manner of its operation, provided that the authority's standing orders have been meticulously followed by the appropriate council resolutions! The district auditor is therefore not a management audit body, although he has powers and influence to draw attention to certain practices which he considers undesirable.

If a ratepayer is going to make representations to the district auditor, the only way he can attain a satisfactory conclusion is by inspecting the accounts in detail. This can be a tremendous task. It must be done during the period that the accounts

are open for public inspection. The problem facing a ratepayer who wishes to make
a representation is, as stated earlier, of knowing when the audit is taking place.

It has been my experience in referring matters to the district auditor outside the
audit periods that he welcomes information concerning council matters. Equally, I
am convinced that he uses his own techniques of investigation to look into the
various matters referred to him, and he is able in some instances to probe into
matters which such submissions bring to light. The answer to a submission may be
a long time coming, but I have no doubt of their professional integrity. However,
I do wish that it was incumbent upon the district auditor to submit a report to the
complainant in a similar manner to that adopted by the ombudsman. It should be
noted that this failure is not due to any negligence by the district auditor, but
due to his statutory duty of reporting on his audit solely to the council. If he
suspects a possible illegality he has the task of passing it over to the police for
them to investigate.

Those who feel sufficiently strongly about bungling or mismanagement should be
prepared to initiate the process of making representations to either the ombudsman
or the district auditor. In both cases, there is a need for as complete a document-
ation as possible to be included in the submission. Where there is a matter which
is appropriate for referring to the district auditor, it is advisable to challenge
an item in the accounts. Every council is bound to give public notice of the audit,
and ratepayers are entitled to inspect the accounts and make copies of any appropriate document as required. If there are, as a result of such investigation, matters
which need attention, the district auditor will carry out his functions and there
will be a formal meeting when the representations are put and the council replies
to them. The district auditor is helpful to those who make representations and
will explain the procedure and, if necessary, the protection available to the ratepayer and when it applies. To inspect the accounts is a process which requires
time and stamina, like all attempts to delve into the bureaucratic machinery to
obtain the necessary information.

However, those who feel aggrieved should not despair too much if the results are
not speedily attained. It is surprising how long these investigations take, even
a simple matter of possible pecuniary interest of a member where there is a
suggestion that it was not declared at the requisite meetings! In spite of the
effort involved in preparing a submission, a reference to the ombudsman or to the
district auditor will cause the authority to look at matters which would otherwise
escape its notice. Any reference, even by a performance review committee, is the
genesis of change. While the person aggrieved may not attain one hundred per cent
success, the effort involved will have its reward in due course.

CHAPTER 14

The Future or Is It Too Late?

There are a large number of very highly skilled professional men in local government whose acumen and dedication is comparable with those in other sectors of the economy. They are exposed to constraints imposed by continuous publicity, and at the same time they have to be entirely free from commercial links, where standards of honesty have slipped alarmingly in recent years. Those who have served as councillors for a time will be able to identify these dedicated public servants. Why is it then that there is so much criticism of the way in which local government is conducted?

The reader will now be aware of the problem of marrying professional skill with managerial ability, and of providing a structure which enables management to function effectively. This is a matter which once recognised is capable of being tackled.

It must not be forgotten that over many decades government, both local and national, has taken over many tasks which were formerly the responsibility of the family, or were undertaken by voluntary societies. The interdependence of the family with its mutual support system has given way to the support system being provided by the State.

Further, where work was undertaken by persons seeking a vocational outlet, it is now performed by persons whose need for employment exerts a stronger pull than the former vocational interest. This is not to argue the merits or demerits of the change, but to emphasise that we now expect local authorities to perform a different role in some fields. Inevitably this has increased their power as well as many people's dependency upon them. In consequence local authorities are more than ever in the public eye.

This exposure to public scrutiny has necessitated strict procedures which tend to the inflexible. As a result, when there are borderline cases where emotion and sympathy call for the intervention of the local authority, but do not seem to fit the tidy administrative guidelines, local government seems to be insensitive.

There is no doubt that when local government was small and personalities meant something and contributed to the 'esprit de corps' of an organisation, the sense of personal involvement and service was a powerful influence which meant something to the locality. It may not have been a highly efficient organisation in economic terms, and often it failed to grapple with the wider issues, but it was highly

sensitive to local reaction. Often the majority of its employees, including the
chief officers, were resident within their respective authorities. Improved travel
facilities has led to aspirants for jobs saying that they can reach the Town Hall
quicker by travelling 30 miles on a motorway link than by travelling across the
town! No longer do local government officers feel it essential to live as well as
work within the community they serve. It is as if they have a special need to
divorce themselves from the influences and pressures of the community. In consequence the responsiveness of local government officers to immediate needs, feelings,
and local pressures is substantially reduced, and the activities from 9 a.m. to
5 p.m. take on those of a routine job in much the same way that most people to to
work in private industry without any sense of involvement in the success of the
business in which they are employed. There are exceptions in both private and
public life, but taken overall they are the exception rather than the rule.

When totalling up the deficit side of the account for local government reorganisation, there will be a substantial item in respect of the loss of the sense of
public service and of the involvement of the public servants in the life of the
community. Whether local government will ever have the courage to make it a con-
dition of service for persons to live within their respective authorities remains
to be seen, yet there are very generous terms available to new appointees to assist
them to move house, and they are more than adequately recompensed for the resultant
disturbance. With state education in a comprehensive form being more universal,
the problems of transferring children should be less than when the educational
structure was more divided. Accordingly it should be relatively easy to make such
conditions of employment effective. The return to a more responsive form of local
administration is the first step needed to offset the present malaise within local
government.

Reorganisation sought to achieve economies of scale. It was an opportunity for
greater professional skills to be available for the benefit of a larger community
than hitherto. Whereas the qualifications of some staff in the smaller authorities
were based upon accumulated experience rather than knowledge gained through training and education, it should now be possible to employ highly-skilled and qualified
persons. Unfortunately structural reorganisation does not provide a change in
human ability. It will be some years before the requisite skills are developed and
deployed. It is a case of waiting for dead mens' shoes.

There is little evidence that the numbers employed by local authorities have decr-
eased due to amalgamations. The provision for no redundancies without very generous severance terms ensured that the possible trend towards manpower reductions
was slow and cumbersome, while the inertia to change ensured that once a post was
established it was difficult to disestablish it. On top of this is the continuous
imposition by central government of additional duties created by the ever-increasing burden of legislation designed to control and direct human activity. So great
has been the effect of legislation that local authorities have assumed the role of
policeman over a wide range of civil conduct, leaving the traditional police force
with the duty of curtailing criminal activity.

While there has been no noticeable change in the manpower resources deployed in the
public sector to achieve this aim of reorganisation, it must not be assumed that
this applies to all authorities. It is a pleasure to report that some authorities
do look very carefully at manning levels, especially when vacancies arise. I have
been a witness to this exercise and it is refreshing to see it in operation. This
is not to assume that because one authority has a lower ratio of staff to ratepayers
that all is well. It often only accentuates the problem which other authorities
face. It is as well to point out at this stage that in conducting reviews of
staffing levels, very seldom is the actual workload set out to enable councillors
to assess whether the organisation matches a reasonable workload.

The requirement in 1976-8 to cut local authority programmes certainly reduced capital expenditure, but it was expected also to reduce revenue expenditure. It failed to achieve the desired aim because of the resistance to manpower cuts to take account of the reduced programme. In many cases it is probably true to say that the cuts resulted in spare capacity in a number of areas - certainly not all. Once the cuts started to be restored as was the case in 1979, the manning levels as at 1977 became the base line for assessment of the staffing/workload ratio needed to cope with the expanding expenditure. The only way that this tendency to increase manning levels can be checked is by the vigilance of the councillors.

The question arises as to whether the councillors are equipped to monitor such a situation. In fact, councillors are often very ill-equipped to do this, because they have to rely on the very same officers, who advocate the increased resource, to provide the data which the councillors must use to challenge the submission. This leads the discussion inevitably to the role of the personnel management funct- ion within an authority. Part of the task of personnel management should be direct- ed towards effective utilisation of manpower resources. Have the personnel depart- ments been given an effective brief on this subject? Have they the requisite skills within the department to fulfil this brief? The answer is naturally mixed, depending on the authority. Firstly, there has been over the years a lack of dev- elopment of personnel management skills within the public sector and local govern- ment is no exception. Where local authorities have been prudent enough to bring in highly skilled persons from outside, the opportunity for effective scrutiny of manpower proposals has increased. Unfortunately the making of appointments is not the complete solution. I have seen such appointments take place, only to find frustration because the officers who head the council's structure and the various departments have been brought up in the traditional local authority environment, and are singularly inexperienced in personnel matters in the modern context. There- fore, however able the person heading the personnel function may be, it is often the case that he or she is thwarted in the task of achieving a worthwhile contrib- ution.

Since the previous chapters have been written, I have had the opportunity to under- take a major review of the personnel management function throughout an authority. It has been a wonderful eye opener to the operation of the council's activities. An examination of the personnel function and its ramifications is the best way of appreciating how local government works. In this instance, there was clearly no corporate policy. Many able administrators were undertaking personnel tasks for which they had never been equipped by experience in depth or by training. In a field where legislation is playing an important part this was a very serious matter and could cause trouble for all councils. Not only that, there was utter confusion about certain basic management matters. For example, there was in some instances open hostility to the use of job descriptions due to the belief that their use would restrict the movement of staff about the office and lead to claims for additional payments. In one case it was held that it would be impossible to transfer someone from highway engineering to drainage work! Such statements indicate that the knowledge of chief officers on the use and value of job descrip- tions, management training programmes and Contracts of Employment were rudimentary.

While the review revealed many discrepancies in practice within the authority, some of which were almost unbelievable against the background of a fervent belief in managerial perfection, there were three areas of major concern which certainly are not confined, I am sure, to the particular authority. The first involved the absence of accountability of managers for the performance of their subordinates. This was revealed in a number of ways; the method of choosing a selection panel for appointments, the lack of any appraisal system after a probationary period or when increments become due, and in a case of an appeal against dismissal the real nigger in the woodpile appeared to be the senior. Incidentally it was discovered later that this senior officer wanted to be moved away from a management role, even with loss of pay, yet no one heeded!

The second area of major concern was the absence of a corporate policy on personnel matters. The major justication of the establishment of a personnel department under the control of the chief executive is the opportunity is provides of ensuring effective use of the council's manpower resources. No chief executive in my judgement should be without this fundamental tool at his command. If this role is not effectively used, it is extremely unlikely that there will be effective control of other aspects of the council's operation, and in particular where the co-ordination function between departments is crucial to the effective completion of a council's programme.

The third, and perhaps the most worrying of all from a councillor's point of view, was the ease with which reports and submissions never see the light of day. These reports may be in draft form from a subordinate on a particular topic, or may be matters which have appeared on the agenda of the management board. The ability of officers to act as an effective screen between the policy makers and those who are entrusted with the preparation of submissions is considerable, and their power is almost absolute. It is even worse in my view when these reports, if acted upon, would have increased the efficiency of the authority. Little wonder, therefore, that there is truth in the statement on the effectiveness of councillors as 'show him round but don't let him see'!

As in all such cases, it is inevitable that those at the top must be held to be accountable for this state of affairs; for no organisation can achieve a level of performance greater than the expectations of the person who wields the greatest power. This is true of elected as well as of paid officials. However, it must be stated in mitigation that those whom one controls and directs as a manager, can by their attitude and behaviou thwart and frustrate the efforts of the senior in post. This is never more so than when a situation of being the senior amongst equals, which existed in the days of Town Clerks, is substituted by a management structure where that senior ceases to be an equal and becomes the chief. In so far as many chief executives have been close associates of departmental heads within the former organisational framework, they often seek to establish their position as the managing director over a period of time. This slow way of developing the chief executive's role may be in tune with the pace of local government, but it fails to seize the opportunity to inject management control and co-ordination afforded by the change in organisational structure. The fact that the change in structure may not suit those who in consequence become subordinate to the chief executive could be construed as providing evidence of a lack of appreciation of the essential management ingredient needed within large scale operations.

It is however not enough to lay the entire blame for the present state of affairs upon the officers. The elected members by and large have themselves not seen the necessity for a change in approach, let alone provided the political will necessary to bring it about. A close inspection of many training programmes since 1974 shows the pre-eminence given to professional training to the almost total exclusion of managerial training. This has been a national disaster to which the cuts in public expenditure have not helped. Where training has been done for instance in the industrial relations field, it has often concentrated on what I can best describe as 'fire brigade' activities. This is particularly true of the area of safety training resulting from the inclusion of local authority activities within the ambit of safety legislation, following the implementation of the Health and Safety at Work etc. Act. Even then, there has often been an absence of a corporate training philosophy. The usual practice is to send the juniors on such courses, while the bosses languish in their ignorance! There is much to be said for the military practice of sending the top brass on a short appreciation course, followed by a slightly longer period for the unit commanders, and the full treatment for those who have to apply themselves to the immediate task for which the training is devised.

If there is to be any fundamental change in the attitude to management training, then as stated in a previous chapter there may have to be government directives to achieve this, unless those who are members of the Association of Chief Executives start to take a lead. No chief executive should be allowed to take up a post unless he has been on a suitable course, such as that run by the Henley College, or is sent on such a course within one year of appointment. Unless it starts at this level there is little hope for any fundamental change taking place which will affect those junior to the chief officer of the authority. Once this happens there will be less reticence in attending courses by departmental chiefs.

It will be appreciated that the opportunity to provide the necessary increased management skills necessary following reorganisation has not been grasped, and not even recognised by many elected members. In consequence, it is necessary to ponder over the problem facing elected members in the whole task of policy direction.

There are many able and community conscious persons who are elected to councils. Many are successful in their own employment situation, but many are unfamiliar with the process of policy formation and implementation which is comparable with that entrusted to the board of directors of a private company. Yet this is the fundamental role of the elected members. Often they are unable to distinguish between the task of managing and of making management accountable to them for performance. Equally they are responsible for seeing that where management is failing, action of whatever kind is taken to remedy the situation. But first of all they have to be able and prepared to identify failure as well as success.

Experience indicates that, because the elected members are the propagandists and the officers the servants of the council with no right of speech in the public forum of the council meeting, the officers are in need of some form of protection from public criticism. It is almost as if the officer can do no wrong. Yet time and again I have listened to senior councillors voice substantial criticism of officers' performance. Yet seldom is any action taken. Not only is there a reluctance to recognise failure, but there is almost an unseemly rush to do 'watergates', and to express in precise terms of a resolution that an officer or department be congratulated on this or that situation which has been the subject of public criticism. The consequence of this is almost to entrench incompetence and failure, and to make possible subsequent disciplinary action more difficult. Should action be needed later on, the well-known method of paying an officer off has to be undertaken at a substantial price, simply because the councillors, as the equivalent of the board of directors, have failed to identify areas of inadequate performance, and so make managers truly accountable.

Time and again, I have seen inadequate management information upon which to make policy decisions. Because an officer has produced a report, it is considered to be the sum total of information, or worse still, to be the correct data upon which to make decisions. Since management accounting is a process seriously underdeveloped within local government in spite of the availability of the computer to produce it, it is little wonder that the officers are able to continue on their present course.

I once challenged a department to provide information about the running of a community venture, having been dissatisfied with the information supplied when the budget for the department was submitted for approval. After further enquiries (the majority party had by this time approved the budget) showed that the running costs for the forthcoming year were to increase by some 5%, while the income was expected to drop by 20%, I requested still further information to show how we might rectify the situation. The result was a long report, giving historical accounting

information which I described as being akin to a 'puff-adding' exercise. There was
no analysis of the charges levied, so that it might be possible to compare costs
and income per hour for each type of letting. The other members of the committee
saw no necessity for this information in order to make decisions as to where the
subsidy from the rates might be provided. The argument was advanced that the
venture provided a community service which required subsidy from the rates! There
were no targets set for achievement by the managers of the venture. It is clear
evidence to my mind that councils concentrate upon a 'puff-adding' exercise to the
exclusion of modern managerial accounting techniques.

The cynic would detect the possibility with the increased subsidy that should the
accounts at the end of the year show that it was not so bad as had been forecast,
there will be congratulations all round! It is not unknown for the budget provisions to be used in this way as a form of self-deception in which councillors and
officers revel!

The democratic process ensures that politically conscious persons are elected, but
if they are, once elected, to perform the proper role as councillors they must
become the equivalent of company directors, ensuring that the managing director and
the management under him performs adequately and that the correct information is
provided to make the policy decisions. Political expertise unfortunately is
unlikely, for reasons which have been stated, to throw up elected members with knowledge and experience in directing organisation. It is equally unfortunate that when
it comes to self-examination politicians are almost totally blind. During my
career as an elected member, I have found few councillors who can detect when the
officers are pulling off confidence tricks or are hiding facts and figures. This
has always concerned me.

No amount of denial of this basic blindness will ever convince me when set against
the welter of facts, many of which have been revealed in this book.

In the absence of persons willing to stand who have managerial experience at this
level, there is an urgent need for the situation to be rectified, even if it means
members going away on short courses. Unless the ratepayers are prepared to pay to
ensure that their councillors have the requisite training, there will be little
change in the quality of local government. If elected members are prepared to do
this, then it is more likely that they will appreciate the need to see that management training is part of the basic requirement of all in senior posts. I suspect
that the absence of effective management training in local government is accepted
by the politicians, who are fearful of power which officers might wield through
being more effective in the management role! If councillors are fearful of this
situation, it will be because they have no recognised means of being trained to
cope with the situation. It would not come amiss for candidates, when giving their
consent to nomination, to give an undertaking to attend special courses for newly
elected members. Some authorities believe that they are providing training by
holding seminars for new members. Unfortunately these seminars are only concerned
with the existing methods of operation, although they do have the additional value
of helping new members assimilate the functions of the various departments and
their respective statutory duties. It is important to speed up the process whereby
new members know their way around, but the seminars do nothing to help them to be
better decision-makers. Like most training within local government, it is in-house
and therefore avoids exposure to external influences. It could be expected that
the Royal Institute of Public Administration would be able to play an important
role in this. Unfortunately this is not the case, having concentrated much of its
previous activity on certain management techniques rather than on developing and
disseminating the results of theoretical and applied research. Regrettably, there
is extremely little of the latter. The Local Government Training Board is not a
suitable candidate for the source of such courses, since it does little to transfer

the expertise of the private sector into the context of public authorities. It might be expected that management consultants should be able to fill the gap. They are possible contributors, but before they do become involved they would have to acquire greater knowledge of the restraints applicable to local government, so that in using their expertise they don't fall into too many traps.

There will be councillors who will deny the necessity for this training, and would contend that by turning their attention towards the management role they would be steering themselves away from the community involvement of local political life. Such councillors overlook the disadvantage in which they are placed when they are required to fulfil their decision msking and controlling role. More important than this, however, is the time required to do this training and its impact upon normal employment. At present they seem incompatible. Time must be allowed for this, and the necessary financial recompense to be available for those who undergo such train- ing. It might not be inappropriate for there to be joint courses of this nature where officers as well as elected members take part in such courses. It would do much to ensure an understanding of the respective roles.

While basic training needs to have the injection of other influences than those of local government, not all training needs to be undertaken by outside agencies. There is expertise available within sections of local authorities on selection procedures, for example. This is an important area calling for improvement of techniques and procedure, as I found when I was recently involved in the selection of a head teacher for an infants school. In order that the reader may be acquaint- ed with the horrific experience, it is worth setting out some of the problems found. Firstly, the education department reproduced on a stencil (rather than a photocopy) the basic details of the application form, and it proceeded to make a precis of the information sent in to support the application. What was formerly two pages of supporting information became in some instances two lines of type- script! Requests for the sight of the full application form at the meeting to agree a short list, as well as before the final interview took place, were refused. Only when the interviews were underway was it possible for any member of the panel to have sight of the full application form. When it was seen, certain facts sub- mitted by the candidates were found not to have been included in the precis. It was also disturbing to have to read a full application form while the other members of the panel were asking questions!

Perhaps the most disturbing feature of the whole process was that other councillors failed to appreciate that anything was wrong! I am not convinced that they were all so naive as to believe that this was the correct way to select for this or any post, although they did point out subsequently to the precedents within the author- ity for selecting teachers in this way! I am sure, however, that a course on inter- viewing techniques would have brought a different perspective to their attention, and brought about changes should such an opportunity ever have been provided. Considering that the elected members have the final say over the most senior of the appointments within the authority, the importance of this task cannot be overstated. If an authority has not got a single individual qualified to train interviewers, then they must seek outside assistance as a matter of urgency, and ensure that such training is provided for both councillors and officers.

If these changes are made, it is doubtful whether it will be tolerable to continue the present system of expecting so many councillors to do so much for so little recompense. The undertaking of a major performance review can involve some thirty to forty hours' work; what time therefore must a chairman of a major committee spend outside the formal meeting to keep abreast of affairs. Some young chairmen of committees have been known to give up their jobs to concentrate on council work, relying on the state to make amends for the time spent in public service. It was quite natural to expect councillors to give freely of their time when authorities were small and intimate, but nowadays councillors are in charge of vast governmental machinery,and they must be able to have time and money to enable them to perform their duties. In some cases chairmen have become almost full time, and to recompense them on the basis of attendance at official meetings is derisory. There is a strong case for some elected members receiving a basic salary. For other members there is a need for greater back-up facilities in secretarial and research areas. We are undoubtedly getting local government on the cheap, as far as elected members are concerned. However hard many of them try, without adequate recompense they cannot devote sufficient time to the preparation and study needed to make effective decisions. What member of the ordinary public will continually have to spend weekends reading reports of up to 70 or more pages? It is not enough to say that the reports are too long. When major reviews of staffing, for example, are involved, all the information has to be there for the councillor to assimilate if he is to take the correct decision. It is easy for the officers who have grown with the development of the proposal. The councillor has the finished document which he has to grasp at a singe meeting within very limited time. For every hour that a councillor has to attend a meeting, he has to spend at least two in preparation, if he or she is to be fully conversant with the subjects under discussion. This time is of course in addition to his constituency work. The dilemma at present is, does the councillor spend all his time amongst his constituents and be seen by them, or does he devote his efforts to ensuring that the council is doing the right things and making the right decisions? The job is too part-time for a councillor who is not retired to do both effectively. The problem is aggravated if you are a member of a minority party, for your resources are often spread too thinly on the ground.

If there was a greater opportunity, as well as facility, for elected members to get to grips with the real problems, rather than the present often cursory attention, the greater would be the likelihood of a better-informed membership. In consequence it might be less likely that decisions would be based on party dogma backed by the party whip.

Has reorganisation really changed things, and is it possible for the potential benefits from economies of scale to be passed on to the ratepayers? The answer to the first question is an emphatic no, while the second still remains a hope, albeit a pious one. This is basically because politicians have failed to understand the change required, but more especially because within the larger units they have concentrated too much on the party political game, to the exclusion of the role entrusted to them to direct and control the performance of the council towards its policy goals. It is of course a reflection on the lack of expertise amongst councillors, and one which can only be overcome by ensuring that competent persons are elected, or by providing an adequate training programme to enable them to perform this duty which all ratepayers wish to see adopted. The failure of democracy lies in its inability to elect persons of known competence, rather than those who are primarily concerned with the trappings of power through political antics.

Let us hope that those who wish to see local authorities become effective and provide value for money will get together and restore some of the benefits of pre-reorganisation with the unrealised potential of the new skills available to us since 1974.